CHURCH
FUND
RAISING

CHURCH BUSINESS MANAGEMENT SERIES

CHURCH FUND RAISING

George W. Harrison

and contributing authors
Howell Farnworth, and
Chester A. Myrom

PRENTICE-HALL, INC.
Englewood Cliffs, New Jersey

Dedicated to
Alice
My Wife
for her patience
and understanding

Library of Congress Catalog Card Number: 64-19677

Printed in the United States of America. T 13373

PRENTICE-HALL INTERNATIONAL, INC., *London*
PRENTICE-HALL OF AUSTRALIA, PTY., LTD., *Sydney*
PRENTICE-HALL OF CANADA, LTD., *Toronto*
PRENTICE-HALL OF INDIA (PRIVATE) LTD., *New Delhi*
PRENTICE-HALL OF JAPAN, INC., *Tokyo*
PRENTICE-HALL DE MEXICO, S.A., *Mexico City*

EDITOR'S INTRODUCTION

THE SERIES of books in which this volume is included was prepared for all who seek new insight and specific guidance in administering business affairs of churches. These books represent the most comprehensive publishing project ever completed in the field of church business management.

Each book in the series is based on two major premises: First, if churches are to accomplish their purposes effectively, their business affairs must be managed as well as, or better than, those of other organizations. Second, since churches are service-rendering rather than profit-making, and because of their voluntary nature and the trustee relationship involved, their business policies and practices must differ in certain respects from those of commercial enterprises—and these differences must be clearly identified and thoroughly understood.

These books are intended (1) to help clergy and laity develop additional competence for effective stewardship of church business responsibilities, (2) to provide stimulation and practical suggestions for professional career employment as business managers of churches and related non-profit organizations, and (3) to make available an educational basis for strengthening the role of pastors as chief administrators of individual churches.

5

In planning, organizing, and evaluating this series of books the editor was confronted with certain basic questions to which explicit answers had not been published. What *is* church business management? What is it *for?* What is it *not?* What is it *not* for? What are its boundaries? The following tentative definition by the editor is the result of his pioneer effort to delineate and identify this field:

> *Church Business Management* is the science and art of administering church program development, financial resources, physical facilities, office services, staff personnel, and public relations—in accordance with the most effective standards of religious stewardship. Included in this concept are such managerial processes as forecasting, planning, organizing, delegating, controlling, evaluating, and reporting. Management of a church's business responsibilities is a facilitating function to be regarded not as an end in itself but as an important means to a worthy end.

Illustrations of what may be considered "church business management" have come from congregations that have added a professional business manager to the employed staff. A carefully-written job description for such a staff member usually can help any church identify the business functions that are essential in establishing and attaining its distinctive purposes. Such job descriptions should, and often do, represent the business manager as a professional consultant and resource leader in helping church officers and staff, both volunteers and employees, perform their administrative duties in relation to the ministry of:

1. *Program Development*—planning, organizing, and scheduling all appropriate means available to the church for achieving its objectives and goals
2. *Financial Management*—budgeting, obtaining, safeguarding, disbursing, and accounting for all financial resources
3. *Property Management*—using, maintaining, and acquiring

physical facilities such as buildings and grounds, furniture, and equipment

4. *Office Management*—providing systematic programs of scheduling, communicating, and recording services to facilitate achievement of administrative functions

5. *Personal Management*—determining and describing staff positions; enlisting, assigning, and training nonprofessional staff, both volunteers and employees; developing and maintaining staff morale

6. *Public Relations*—communicating the church's concept of its purposes, its programs, its accomplishments, its potentialities, and its needs

Church business management as viewed in this light, and when applied creatively through proper use of collaborative and democratic procedures, is a significant phase of a meaningful spiritual ministry. How successfully and effectively the author of each book in this series has amplified the foregoing philosophy and specifications each reader will, of course, judge for himself.

For invaluable advice and practical assistance throughout the planning and execution stages of this endeavor the editor is especially grateful to Dr. Nathan A Baily, Dean of American University's School of Business Administration. Dean Baily's keen interest and able leadership stimulated the establishment of The American University Center for Church Business Management while facilitating the development of this series of books.

Clyde W. Humphrey
General Editor

Washington, D. C.

PREFACE

THE SUBJECT with which this book is concerned
has a beginning but no ending. It began in prehistoric days
when man paid tribute to his gods with whatever was available. The end is not yet in sight, for as long as man worships
his Creator through the medium of organized religion he
will *need money*. Since there is never enough money to do
what man wishes to do for his God and for his fellowman
there will always be the need for fund raising.

The approach in this book is more than materialistic, however. Time after time it is pointed out that dollars and cents
are not the ultimate goal. These are the media through
which we get the donor to make a deeper commitment of
himself. Most people follow their dollars with keen interest.
If the giver makes a sacrificial gift he is more likely to give
himself unstintingly.

The church should have good business management but
it is more than a business. A business is run for profit. A
church is not! The money a church receives is to be used
for others. It is to be given away that others may benefit
therefrom.

Church fund raising is not only to benefit the giver and
others, but also to bring honor to God. In giving money to

8

the church we are placing our tributes of love and devotion on the altar in reverence to God.

The approach in this book, therefore, is to recognize that we are dealing with the mundane, the materialistic, but to elevate it to a place of spirituality.

Much has been written about certain phases of church-fund raising—tithing, pledging, building funds, etc. But in this book we have devoted whole chapters to such things as the sale of bonds, how to make loans and a greatly neglected area of church finances—wills and bequests. The hope is that others may be encouraged to do much more research and development in these subjects.

I readily admit there are areas of controversy in some of these phases of fund raising. This is as it should be. The rubbing of mind against mind sharpens both.

Several revolutionary changes in raising money for churches have been suggested in the chapter on pledges. In the past 25 years many changes have taken place in the methods of church fund raising. It is possible there will be many more changes in the next 25 years.

This book is meant for both pastors and laymen. It may be used in large and small churches. The ideas and suggestions are adaptable to any situation.

I acknowledge my indebtedness to the innumerable laymen with whom I have been associated through the years, to the many churches in which it has been my privilege to serve either as pastor or director of every-member visitations and to the many people from whom I have gathered illustrations and personal experiences in the area of church finance.

I am deeply indebted to two co-laborers who have assisted in writing this book: Chester A. Myrom, executive director, United Lutheran Church Foundation, an agency of The United Lutheran Church in America, 231 Madison Avenue, New York 16, New York—Mr. Myrom wrote chapter 5, "Deferred Giving: a New Dimension on Christian Steward-

ship." Howell Farnworth, Falls Church, Virginia, president
of Agne-Farnworth Associates, directors of church fund
raising canvasses—Mr. Farnworth contributed much to
Chapter 7, "Knowing Your Destination."

I want to pay tribute to my wife, who gave much assistance in typing the manuscript and in showing much understanding during the many hours that were given to the
preparation of the book.

CONTENTS

Chapter 1

CHURCH MONEY

MONEY is *not* the root of all evil. Some say it is but they do not mean what they say. It is a tongue-in-cheek expression.

These people are like the young minister who condemned air-conditioning in churches because to him it represented deterioration in religion and made Christians soft. Yet, when he had an opportunity to serve an air-conditioned church he did so. So there are those who condemn money while envying those who possess it. Yet these same people are not averse to taking an increase in salary or investing where the returns are profitable.

Money is used to cause evil. With it one may bribe officers of the law, corrupt justice, seduce humanity, pervert government and demoralize whole societies. But none of these prove that money is the root of evil.

Money is neither good nor evil. It is amoral—a neutral object. Money is a means to an end in that it represents many other things. Therefore, money can be used for either good or evil. It is like the rays of the sun, which while falling upon one place cause it to blossom into a delightful garden, but while falling into another place cause barrenness and desert.

Money is not the root of all evil. It is the *love* of money that causes the trouble. Here is where personality comes into the picture, for it is the individual who makes money good or evil. The moral value of money depends on the use that is made of it.

GOD'S MONEY

The money about which we are speaking is that which has come into the hands of those devoted to God. The money might have been used for some immoral or illegal purpose. But now it is in the possession of one who loves God and His Church. The money is then given to the work of God through some church, or some church agency, with the desire that it be used for accomplishing much good locally or universally. This money becomes "church money." Perhaps we could call it "God's money." Thus, it becomes a means for accomplishing good.

In speaking of "money" we do not mean just dollars and cents. These are the most common media of exchange. But we must consider, also, such things as legacies, insurance, wills, endowments, stocks, bonds or any other form of exchange that represents wealth in our economy. The term "money," as used in this book, implies nearly all forms of wealth.

We must adopt a loftier concept of "church money." Loftier both in terms of moral accomplishments through money and in terms of amount of money. We must think in terms of the banker, the investment broker, the trust officer. These people look on money as the power that makes the wheels of business, industry and government move. Money represents man power, it is the result of use of brain and brawn. Money is the seed that is planted today and brings forth the businesses and the banks and the houses of tomorrow. In addition to these, however, the banker, the investment broker, the trust officer think in terms of much money.

They talk in terms of hundreds of thousands of millions of dollars for their purposes. It seems to me, therefore, that we who are representative of the greatest government in time or eternity, the Kingdom of God, and are charged with the greatest business in the world, that of saving the souls of mortal men, must think as big as do those who represent earthly governments and who are interested in undertakings far less important than that with which we are charged.

Small-change ideas must not prevail when considering church money. The reason we have accomplished so little for God and for His Church is that we have conditioned ourselves to think small and to expect small. We have been extremely successful in attaining our small goals! And the success has come because we have been satisfied with nickels (which are of little value anywhere else except in church), dimes and quarters. The time is long past when we should have raised our vision in "church money" to talk big, to think big and to expect big!

The narrow vision we have in our adulthood pertaining to "church money" is a carry-over from our training as children. During our growing up we were taught that the church was a nickel or dime institution. Our parents did not tell us this openly. It was inferred by the amount of money they gave us to drop in the Sunday school offering. Then when we began to give through the church envelope as young people, we were still giving dimes or maybe quarters. As time passed and we became adults earning our own living and establishing our own homes, many never advanced beyond the 5-cent to 25-cent phase of giving through the church.

It is interesting to note, however, that during this same time we were having to pay more to get into places of amusement or to ride on means of public transportation. We were becoming adults in these areas of life but remaining children in our relationship to the church.

SHALL A MAN TIP GOD?

If religion is to combat atheism, we must stop both tipping
God and being satisfied with a tip for God. Some years ago
while dining in a restaurant in Winnipeg, Canada, I saw a
waitress become very angry because of the small tip which
had been left on her table. She had given excellent service
to a family of four. The father of the family had not been
very pleasant with the waitress during the meal. She tried
to be prompt and to pacify a disgruntled customer. But when
the family left, the father put a penny on the table for the
waitress. Fortunately, she did not discover the coin until the
family had pulled out of the parking lot. If she could have
found the man there might have been a fatherless family.
She was angry, not only at the amount left but because she
felt it an insult to her work.

How many times have we given such a tip to God? We
expect Him to be satisfied and at the same time to make sure
we are properly cared for. Tips are not enough.

One reason we support our religion with tips is that it has
a very minor place in our lives. We have relegated it to a
place where we can put up with it or do without it, depending on the circumstances. Of course, this is not true of every-
body, but to the bulk of church members the accusation
cannot be denied.

This was brought to focus during the Century 21 World's
Fair at Seattle, Washington. Hundreds of thousands stood in
line for hours to see some of the science exhibits, or to take
a pseudo-travel through space or to see the latest projected
developments in travel and communications. But the numbers who entered the Christian religious exhibit, provided by
the churches of Seattle, were comparatively insignificant.
Millions of dollars had been spent to show the latest scientific developments and their benefits to man, but a paltry
widow's mite, in comparison, had been collected and spent

to show the effect of religion, particularly Christianity, in our lives.

So goes the story of religion as a whole. It is a necessity at birth, marriage and death. But during the rest of the cycle we seem to think we can manage well without it. Because of this attitude toward our religion, we are satisfied to tip God and His Church.

Another reason we tip God through church giving is that so many other agencies are doing work which was once ascribed to the church. The missionary program of the church has suffered great loss of prestige through the Peace Corps organization of the government. Tax money is used to support workers in areas where the church at one time sent its representatives. Or, look at the list of agencies helped by the United Givers Fund or the Community Chest. Almost every one of them is doing work, and good work, among people and in needs where the church one time functioned. As a result, the church is being squeezed into a narrower and narrower niche in the affairs of life. Since we are expected to financially support these worthy groups, our giving to God through the church has been decreasing until much giving is only to be classed as a tip.

CHURCH BUSINESS

We must raise money for the church, large amounts of it, and we must do it in a businesslike manner. To some, both of these ideas are bad: money is evil and business procedures in the church are just as evil. Some seem to believe that the only Christian way to raise church funds is to receive money only during the worship service, accepting whatever people are willing to give. All other practices are out of place and sinful. Some believe there is no place for planned canvasses, purposeful budgets, prescribed programs. All of these efforts quench the motivation of the Holy Spirit, we are told.

One minister, who is very much interested in church man-

agement and businesslike methods in the church, attended a
meeting of clergymen in a metropolitan area to explain to
them an institute that was to be held in their city pertaining
to church administration, including this subject of fund raising. After the meeting he stood at the door to distribute
literature about the institute. Several of the ministers passed
him by, rudely shunning his efforts. They told him they
wanted nothing to do with such a project because it was
uncalled for and certainly out of place in the work of the
church. If they could not depend on God to take care of the
material things in the church, then something was wrong
with their religion.

I am reminded of a couple who were members of what
they called a "free worshiping" church, visiting in a church
which used liturgy. As the couple looked around, they noticed a hymn board in the front of the nave on which were
the numbers of the hymns that had been used the previous
Sunday. They said to the minister, "Do you choose the hymns
before the service?" He replied that he did. They were quite
surprised and said, "Do you not realize that is opposed to
the working of the Holy Spirit? The hymns should be chosen
as the Spirit leads."

So there are those who state that planned programs and
planned financial efforts are opposed to the free working of
the Holy Spirit in the hearts of worshipers and church members. With this we do not agree.

The Spirit of God can as easily motivate a person to sign
a pledge card in his own home to help underwrite a budget
that has been thoroughly thought out as He can motivate
one to give on the spur of the moment. In fact, the gift is
more likely to be given with more love and greater devotion
after the donor has had time to think about it than if he did
give under the impulse of some emotional appeal. Planning
and order is more Godlike than thoughtlessness and confusion.

MONEY IS NECESSARY

This book is devoted primarily to one facet of the total work of church administration: that of raising money for the church. Without money, what would we administer? Without money, where would we serve? Without money, what would we build? Without money, whom would we educate? Without money, how would we heal? Money is the fuel that keeps the motor running; it is the power that thrusts the church into a place in the world where it will do most good. As much as one may close his eyes to this whole fact, money remains an ultimate necessity. This cannot be denied.

The insurance company for which I worked some years ago had a loan office adjacent to the sales office. Representatives in the loan office made loans on real estate developments, new apartment buildings and other such investments. However, they took the attitude that their work was much more dignified and had higher status than the work done by the sales force. They were reduced to size when it was pointed out to them that unless the salesmen were out knocking on doors and busy on the telephone cultivating prospects and selling insurance, thereby bringing in money for the company, there would be no money to lend. They would soon be out of a job.

Such financing is needed also in the church. Unless money is brought into the church, unless we are concerned about fund raising, then we can close the doors of the church or the creditors will do it for us.

BUT MONEY IS NOT EVERYTHING

Some of the foregoing statements may seem cold and unfeeling. However, let me emphasize, as churchmen we are still involved in one of the greatest spiritual projects on this earth. We may become so concerned about raising funds that we lose sight of the primary purpose of the church and its duty before God. We are to evangelize, to make disciples of all peoples, to preach the gospel as it is in Jesus, the Christ. This we cannot and dare not overlook. In the process of fund raising for the church we are also assuming our greater spiritual responsibilities.

While raising money for the church we should also be endeavoring to deepen the spiritual lives of men and women and youth. It is not enough to have people dedicate their money to the work of God through His Church. We must have the offerer dedicate himself to God in a deeper and newer way.

We called on a prominent businessman in California to ask his help in a financial drive for his church. We wanted his money, certainly, but we wanted him, too. He was very frank in stating he had not been to a worship service for years. He had shown no interest in the church, although he had allowed his name to be kept on the rolls. We knew this before we went to talk to him. This did not matter. This man was needed for the work of the Kingdom of God. We discussed the project with him for some time before he consented to assume an important post in the undertaking. He used his whole office staff in preparing letters and brochures, he gave hours of his busy time, he conferred with others who had not been very active in their church, but, most of all, he gave himself. He returned to his church and dedicated himself to the work of the Lord.

MONEY REPRESENTS THE GIVER

We must raise money, but let us remember that money represents the giver: his strength, his wisdom, his talents, his time, his energies. When his money is placed on the altar of the church, or dedicated in any other way, he is giving himself.

People must know that when they underwrite the erection

of a church edifice, they are leaving a great heritage. When they remember the church in their wills, they are extending themselves into the future far beyond the short time they live on this earth. We want them to know that when they give their money to God, through His Church, they are baptizing their worldly goods with an eternal power that will set forces in motion which will run into the endless future.

Though we may raise money in a cold, factual manner, we are nevertheless quite aware of the spiritual overtones of our undertaking. In all things we must bring men and women to a deeper understanding of themselves and to a more profound dedication to God.

OFFERINGS, NOT COLLECTIONS

Another matter needs to be brought to our attention. It is trifling, but annoying. To my mind, it is improper and lacking in spirituality to receive a "collection" for God or for His Church. We receive "offerings." Collections are taken for neighborhood acts of kindness, such as purchasing flowers for someone ill. Collections are taken for charitable purposes, as for the Red Cross, United Givers Fund or a Volunteer Fire Company. We collect money to give a gift to a departing co-worker. But when the ushers pass the offering plates during a worship service, they are not collecting money. When people are asked to give their money during the Sunday school session, they should not be told it is a collection. Furthermore, the cards which show the amount received in Sunday school and which hang so prominently in our churches as if they were objects of worship, should not read "Amount of Collection Today." These are offerings!

God is not a merchant who sells his goods to the public on installments and, if the installments are delinquent, sends "collectors" out to get what is due Him. He is not a lender of money who takes promissory notes for what is due

Him and, if the notes are overdue, sends someone to "collect" for Him. "Collections" are out of place in worship services and Sunday school classes.

It is true that we owe God a portion of what we have. In fact, it all belongs to Him. However, if we withhold for our own purposes what should be given to God, He will not send "collectors." God loves a cheerful giver. To give under pressure or after our arm has been twisted does not make us cheerful. My feeling is that God would prefer to do without. However, our offerings are an honor to God and reflect the proper spirit of our giving.

We receive "offerings" for God. When the plates are passed in a worship service they are "offering" plates. When adults, youths, boys and girls give their money in the Sunday school, it is not a Sunday school "collection," but an "offering" to God.

When we refer to the Old Testament, the concept of offering becomes quite clear. To the nomads, around whom the Old Testament is centered, money was an unknown quantity as a medium of exchange. The products of their hands were sheep, cattle, doves, pigeons, wheat, barley and such other things which we associate with a rural economy. When these people worshiped God they brought their products with them. These were given to the priest who in turn offered them on the altar before God. The livestock was slain and the meat burned over the fire. The fruit and the vegetables were disposed of in other ways. But all of these were made as offerings. They were not collections. For with the rising of the smoke and odor, rose the prayers and devotions of the offerers.

We do not live in a rural economy. We sell our services and our skills and in return are paid in dollars and cents. When we worship God, we bring dollars and cents which represent our labors, our fruits and the sweat of our brow.

They are placed on the altar of the church through the priestly act of the clergyman as our offering to God. We do not collect, we offer.

MONEY—A SENSITIVE SUBJECT

As we further consider the matter of church money, our offerings to God, the necessity of obtaining funds and all that money means to extending the Kingdom of God, we wonder why ministers and laymen are so sensitive to the mention of money as it relates to the church. A touchy nerve extends from the ears to the wallet or purse. With the mention of money from the pulpit, there are paroxysms of fear which lead to shudders of anger which ultimately cause complete paralysis of the giving hand. In fact, some readers may never reach this point in this book because they may feel writing or talking about money for the church is sacrilegious and unnecessary.

A few people object to sermons on the subject of money. A person will sit through a sermon in which his pastor may denounce the grossest sins or attack some current social problem. He will commend his pastor for his stand and promise him his loyal support. He will tell his neighbors what a courageous person his pastor is. But when his pastor speaks about money or the individual's stewardship, the pastor's halo begins to fade. Frequently the very loudest supporter of the church is its greatest critic when finances are mentioned. He says it is time for the preacher to stop talking about money and return to the gospel.

The backwoods preacher one day got warmed up denouncing the evils of the day. He condemned smoking. One lady sitting down front said, "That's preaching, brother." He denounced movie-going. She said, "That's right, brother." He deplored card playing. She said, "Amen, brother, you tell them." He finally got around to condemning gossiping. Then she turned and said, "Now he's left preachin' and gone to meddlin'." Sometimes the minister is scolded for meddling when he talks about money.

Many members of churches are thin-skinned when asked to help support the church. One family united with a church in what appeared to be good intent. They were enthusiastic about their uniting and it seemed they would be a real asset to the group. But, sadly, the seed was sown on shallow ground. A few weeks after they became members of the church, the quarterly financial statements were mailed to all members. This family received one. The father was immediately offended. He said the church was dunning him. He complained that his name had not even dried on the church records before he was reminded of his financial obligation. The family never returned.

The part of this story that is difficult to understand is that this man had joined a fraternal organization about the same time he had united with the church. To get into this fraternity he was told how much he would have to pay, even before his name would be considered. Then, if he were accepted, he would have to pay a specified amount before he could be initiated. Each year thereafter he received a bill *telling him* to pay his dues. This procedure did not offend him at all!

One often wonders just how the church is to survive. It must be divinely instituted for it seems that in many instances it survives only by the grace of God. Perhaps as indicated earlier, money is dirty—even dirtier than sin—and should not be mentioned from the pulpit. Yet, Jesus talked more about money and its use than about any other subject. He was well aware of its power, both for good and for evil.

Perhaps the reluctance of both ministers and laymen to discuss church money accounts for the fact that so little has been written about it. In most books on church business management there is a chapter on the every-member canvass. A great deal has been written about tithing because of the reawakening of interest in the subject. In more recent years denominational boards have become aware of wills and legacies as a means of church income. A few writers have done some research on "gimmicks" in fund raising. Nevertheless, there is a paucity of material in the total and broader aspect of church fund raising.

I have had a keen interest in this subject of church fund raising for a good many years. The scarcity of material written on it was brought to focus when I became associated with the Center for Church Business Management, The American University, Washington, D.C.

In doing research to bring together material to present to the discussion groups, I found one author after another writing about the every-member canvass and its organization, but little more. I realized that few persons had taken time to get down to the broader problems of church financing.

In this book we have merely scratched the surface. Beyond the pages of this volume lies a deep, untouched mine that will surrender its riches to those who search. Some of what is presented here is the result of hours of discussion with laymen and clergymen in study groups sponsored by the Center for Church Business Management. Some comes from personal experiences. Some is by men who are specialists in their fields.

This book is presented as a pilot attempt in an important subject. It is hoped that others will be challenged to build on these meager foundations to bring the whole subject to further maturity.

Chapter 2

TO TITHE OR NOT TO TITHE

TITHING has had a long and frequently an inglorious history. Like the ebb and flow of the ocean, tithing has risen in popularity only to sink again to the depths of disgrace. At times churchmen have sung its praises and have sought God's favor by making tithing the measure of giving. Other times churchmen have scoffed at tithing, stating that it spoils the spirit of voluntary giving and becomes a tax. Tithing has been called a questionable means of church fund raising. It has been shunned as an affront to God. In our time tithing has returned to a place of prestige. In general, this has been the history of tithing.

PRE-BIBLICAL HISTORY

In more detail, I think of the history of tithing as a path which starts before the Bible came into being, cuts through the Bible and eventually emerges from the Bible again. Sometimes the path is easy to follow. At other times it grows hazy. Occasionally it is lost to sight completely and must be picked up farther along.

The authors of the Bible were influenced by the Egyptians. Naturally they adopted some of the practices and social customs of the people among whom they lived. One of these customs was tithing. As early as 3000 B.C. the Egyptians paid tithes to their war gods. They believed the gods were their partners in war. If the Egyptians were victorious in conflict, then the war gods received a tithe of the spoils of war.

Herodotus, the earliest Greek historian, is credited with the information that Cyrus, king of Persia, 559 B.C., encouraged his soldiers to contribute one-tenth of their spoils of war to their supreme deity. There was a sinister motive behind this request. Cyrus requested one-tenth be given to the god in order to keep any one of his soldiers from becoming wealthier than Cyrus himself. The offerings to the deity were in reality offerings to Cyrus.

The annals of other nations such as Babylon, Phoenicia, Arabia, Carthage, China, Greece and Rome indicate that tithes were given to the gods of these people. This is an interesting fact in the history of tithing because it reveals that tithing was not an innovation of the Biblical people. It had its roots back in the hazy dawn of history.

OLD TESTAMENT TITHING

The first tither in the Bible is Abraham. Abraham was returning from a victorious battle in which he had rescued his nephew Lot and family. On his return home Abraham was met by the mysterious priest, Melchizedek. Abraham offered to this priest one-tenth of "all" that he had. This is the only record of Abraham tithing! Although no further evidence is given, the silence may infer that tithing was such a common practice with Abraham that no further mention was necessary.

The next tither in the Bible is Jacob, the grandson of Abraham. Jacob was running away from home in fear. He had come into disfavor with his father and into disrepute with his brother. With the help of his mother, he was escaping to a strange land to live among strange people. Night came on him in a lonely place. As Jacob slept, he had a vision of God. When Jacob awoke he was both frightened and

pleased. He interpreted his dream to mean that God would
be with him. Jacob made this covenant with God, "Of all
that thou shalt give me, I will surely give the tenth unto
thee." Jacob tithed and God prospered him.

After this the path becomes hazy. There is a great deal of
confusion here in following the history of tithing. Some Biblical authorities state there were three basic religious tithes.
Others state the tithes represented three stages of development in the history of the Israelites. Although the path is
difficult to follow, and sometimes becomes lost completely,
we will consider the tithe as recorded in the priestly codes
and Mosaic regulations.

The first account of tithing in Mosaic regulations is recorded in Numbers 18:20-32. This was an annual tithe for
the support of the Levites who, being the spiritual servants
of the people, were not permitted to till the soil or to become
herdsmen. Consequently, they were dependent on the tithes
brought by the people. In turn the Levites were required to
pay a tithe of their tithe. This was for the support of the
high priest and his associates.

A second annual tithe was required according to Deuter-
onomy 14:22-27. This tithe was brought to a nationwide
religious festival as an offering to God. If the giver lived close
enough to the festival he brought his tithe (of livestock) to
the festival and ate it in the presence of the Lord. If, however, he lived too far away so there was the possibility of his
tithe (of livestock) spoiling or perishing enroute to the place
of the festival, he could convert the tithe into money and,
after arriving at the festival, purchase a desired animal to
contribute.

Every third year another tithe was required. This tithe was
in addition to the two annual tithes already mentioned. It
was designated for the care of the needy. "And the Levite
. . . and the stranger, and the fatherless, and the widow,

which are within thy gates, shall come, and shall eat and be satisfied; that the Lord thy God may bless thee in all the work of thine hand which thou doest" (Deut. 14:28, 29).

It is important to note that the Israelites gave *tithes,* not a tithe. One can imagine the financial burden the ecclesiastical organization put on these people. Even more amazing is the fact that this 30 percent was only a part of their total giving. When Moses gave the laws concerning offerings and festivals he wrote, "And thither ye shall bring your burnt offerings, and your sacrifices, and your tithes, and heave offerings of your hand, and your vows, and your freewill offerings, and the firstlings of your herds and of your flocks" (Deut. 12:6). Go back and read these instructions again—then note, these offerings were *in addition* to the tithes.

In this maze of laws and codes the path of tithing is lost in confusion. There is no unanimity of thought by Biblical authorities. It is believed that both David and Solomon used the tithe as a means of supporting their governments.

Tithing is mentioned only sporadically by the prophets. For instance, Amos talks about it but with sarcasm. He condemns the people for their sinning and injustices while at the same time offering tithes to God. Some centuries later, Nehemiah encouraged the people to bring their tithes to help rebuild the wall at Jerusalem. A contemporary of Nehemiah, Malachi, tried to rebuild the faith of the people. One of the reasons he gave for their weak faith was that they had failed to tithe and thus robbed God.

JESUS AND TITHING

We come to the New Testament. Our concern here is principally with what Jesus did, and said, about tithing. If only there were some specific quotation to which we could point and say, "That is it!" Unfortunately, there is no such conclusive statement from Jesus about tithing.

On two occasions Jesus said something about tithing. In both of these instances His remarks were negative. One refers to the Pharisee praying in the temple. "Two men went up into the temple to pray: the one a Pharisee, and the other a publican. The Pharisee stood and prayed thus with himself, God, I thank thee, that I am not as other men *are*, extortioners, unjust, adulterers, or even as this publican. I fast twice in a week, I give tithes of all that I possess. And the publican, standing afar off, would not lift up so much as *his* eyes unto heaven, but smote upon his breast, saying, God be merciful to me a sinner. I tell you, this man went down to his house justified *rather* than the other . . ." (Luke 18:10-14).

The other relates to the habits and attitudes of the Pharisees. "Woe unto you, scribes and Pharisees, hypocrites! for ye pay tithe of mint and anise and cummin, and have omitted the weightier *matters* of the law, judgment, mercy, and faith: these ye ought to have done, and not to leave the other undone" (Matt. 23:23).

Only by conjecture can we say Jesus was a tither. He was a devotee of the Jewish religion. As such, he adhered to the practices of his people. If his people tithed then no doubt he did also. We can merely surmise.

Beyond these two references, nothing about tithing is recorded in the New Testament. Either the writers, including St. Paul, took tithing as a commonplace practice, or they considered it so unimportant they wrote nothing about it.

POST-BIBLICAL TITHING

The path of tithing emerges from the Bible. We come to post-Biblical times. The Christians in the first two centuries heard and knew little of tithing. Giving was voluntary, based on the believer's gratitude to God for deliverance from sin through the cross.

In the third century, however, there is a change in attitude.

Tithing began to be stressed. There was a great need to provide for both the clergy and the poor—and frequently the argument turned on the question of who should have preference, the clergy or the poor.

After this, more and more emphasis is placed on tithing. Higher and higher authorities favored the practice. First, theologians such as Jerome, Ambrose, Augustine and Chrysostom made tithing the themes of their sermons. Congregations were both threatened and cajoled. Eventually tithing was made official by the Council of Tours and the second Council of Macon. By the ninth century, the tithe became civil law in the West.

With the rise of the papacy and its struggle with the civil governments, the history of tithing enters another period of confusion. It is not our purpose to go into closer detail of this period so we will pick up the path nearer our own time.

TITHING RESURRECTED

Within the last one hundred years tithing has had a resurrection! It has come forth to give new life to many Christians and new vigor to many churches. This time the motivation has come from the laity and not from councils, religious authorities or clergy disputants. The laymen have passed the word that God will prosper those who honor Him with a tenth of their income. Along with words, evidence has been given that "it works."

Perhaps the most prominent layman in the tithing movement was Thomas Kane, 1876. In fact, if there were a "Mister Tither" he would hold the title. Thomas Kane was a Chicago businessman who recognized tithing as a basis for material prosperity. In fairness to Mr. Kane, it must be admitted he did not advocate tithing for this purpose. Nevertheless, he noticed that after practicing tithing for some time his business did prosper. His curiosity was aroused about the

benefits of tithing, so he began to make inquiry among other
business acquaintances who he knew were tithing. They
gave the same testimony he did.

Mr. Kane then wrote about the benefits of tithing in a
pamphlet, which was distributed to the majority of Protestant
ministers in the United States in order to solicit their support.
The result was the formation of The Layman Company,
which dedicated itself to encouraging tithing among church
members and distributed millions of pamphlets and tracts on
the subject.

Another boost to tithing came through William G. Roberts,
an attorney and the treasurer of Wesley Chapel Methodist
Episcopal Church in Cincinnati, Ohio. During the year 1895
this church struggled to meet its financial obligations. Regardless of what was done it was not enough. Mr. Roberts
challenged his fellow members to tithe. The results were so
spectacular that other churches did the same. Tithing was
taking hold and people were learning its possibilities.

DENOMINATIONAL TITHING

Although tithing was made prominent by Kane and Roberts, others had already been using it as a means of church
finance. Since 1838 some denominations have encouraged,
and almost demanded, their constituents to tithe. As the
financial success of these denominations became known,
others endorsed tithing. The Church of Jesus Christ of Latter-
day Saints officially endorsed tithing in 1838. They were followed by the Seventh-day Adventists in 1863. Then came the
Salvation Army and the United Presbyterian Church in 1865.
The United Brethern in Christ was next in 1889. Two years
later, 1891, the Presbyterian Church in the U.S. gave official
endorsement to tithing. The Southern Baptist Convention
followed suit in 1894. Since the turn of the century, eighteen
other denominations in the United States have officially sanc-
tioned tithing.

Typical of the attitude of denominations to the tithing is that of The Methodist Church. In 1939 when the Methodist Episcopal Church, the Methodist Episcopal Church, South, and the Methodist Protestant Church united, there was no mention of tithing, at least not on record. Since that time The Methodist Church in *The Discipline of The Methodist Church* has had this to say about tithing: In 1940—"The dedication of the tenth of income offers a basic principle of beneficence supported by centuries of religious custom and joyful experience" (#1249). Four years later this is recorded —"Tithing is commended as a historic and workable method attested by many Christians throughout centuries of religious custom and joyful experience" (#223). In 1952 the language is stronger—"Stewardship of possessions shall be interpreted to mean that the tithe is the minimum standard of giving for Methodist people, and shall be promoted by the above agencies [meaning Education and Lay Activities] by providing appropriate literature for the use of churches and pastors in enlisting Methodist people as tithers" (#753). The sense of this statement has not been changed since that time.

In the meantime, however, The Methodist Church has emphasized tithing through literature, conferences and promotion. Recently, one whole year was devoted to an emphasis on tithing.

This brief historical background gives some understanding of the roots of tithing. Now we come to our own day and time, and endeavor to determine what tithing may mean to us.

LAW VERSUS GRACE

In my opinion we are faced with one of two basic options. We may become dogmatic and legalistic, insisting that God specifically and clearly states we can do no less than tithe— and that means give one-tenth! This argument is based on Malachi 3:10, "Bring ye all the tithes into the storehouse, that there may be meat in mine house, and prove me herewith, saith the Lord of hosts, if I will not open you the windows of heaven, and pour you out a blessing, that there shall not be room enough to receive it."

Or, the alternative is that we present our tithes motivated by the love of Jesus Christ. We, being the benefactors of His unselfishness, will share spontaneously and lovingly whether it is a tithe, more than a tithe or less than a tithe. This argument is based on II Corinthians 8:9, "For ye know the grace of our Lord Jesus Christ, that, though he was rich, yet for your sakes he became poor, that ye through his poverty might be rich."

If every Christian family in the United States tithed, the power of Christianity would be felt with such magnitude that the whole world would be affected. Considering it from a purely materialistic point of view, there is no more lucrative a manner of raising money for the church than by tithing. It would solve many problems and reduce many annoyances. There would be no need for every-member canvasses, nor for gadgets and gimmicks. Many questionable methods of raising money would become obsolete if people called Christians would tithe.

The very mathematics of tithing supports the conviction that other fund-raising methods are unnecessary. Let us assume there is a church of one hundred member-families consisting of two adults and one child between the ages of 7 and 12. Let us further assume that these are receiving public welfare, without any other income. If they tithe, they could support a church financial program of $20,000 a year. Think of this: a church whose membership is wholly on public welfare supporting a $20,000 budget—all because they tithe their poverty!

To be sure this is strictly hypothetical. We are stating that, mathematically, if people tithe, regardless of how low the income, the results are amazing.

Let us consider another church, the same size. According to authorities the average income per family in this nation is $5,000. Assuming we have a church of one hundred member-families with the national average income, they could support a $50,000 per year financial program, if all members tithe.

Take out your own pencil and do some similar figuring for your own church and learn what the giving potential really is.

OBJECTION TO LEGALISTIC TITHING

There is no substitute for tithing in church fund raising. It is the easiest and the most productive method of financing the Christian program. In spite of this, there are more objections to this procedure than to any other suggested method. Why? I do not claim to have the only answer but I have one: I believe many people object to tithing because it has been legalized! Many church members have been led to believe that tithing is not a matter of grace nor of the believer's love for God through Jesus, the Christ. They have been told "tithing is the law of God. If you do not obey this law, if you rob God by giving Him less than a tenth, then do not expect God to give you His full blessing." To this, some conscientious churchmen object, and I join them. We do not want to be bound by law again after having been set free from the law through Christ. What the Christian does, he should do out of love and with joy.

I am opposed to tithing if it is imposed on Christians by dogmatic and dictatorial statements. One of the basic tenets of Protestantism is freedom of worship and freedom in our expressions of worship. As Protestants we do not want to be told what church we must attend, what forms of worship we are to use, to what creeds we must subscribe nor how much of our time or our money we should give to God through the church.

Thus, when some ecclesiastical authority tells us we *must*

give a tithe, it ceases to be an offering! It becomes a tax! To this we object because we moved out of the tax status in our support of the work of God through the church when we established the philosophy of separation of state and church.

Furthermore, I am opposed to tithing when we are told it is the *only* measure by which we may judge our offerings to God. "Tithing is a must, anything beyond that is our offering," we are told. The widow's offering was only a fraction of a penny, but Jesus commended her for it. Was it a tithe? Zaccheus made restitution to all those whom he had wronged. Jesus commended him for it. Was it a tithe? When a bed-fast shut-in puts fifty cents into the hands of her pastor and requests him to put it in the offering plate, he would be out of order if he told her that unless it was a tithe it would not be acceptable before God.

Jesus said nothing about the magnificent gifts given by the more prosperous people. It was not the size of the gift but the spirit in which it was given that meant so much to Him.

I believe there are other formulae which may be used in measuring our giving to God. St. Paul's statement, that we give as God has prospered us, is a real challenge. Of course, we may rationalize out of this point of view by stating we have not prospered. There are always those ahead of us who seem to have more, and compared to them we have little. However, at the same time there are many behind us who do not have what we have. Prosperity becomes a relative thing. But no matter how we measure it, whatever we have we owe to God.

Another formula which has been of great value to many families is to give $1 per week for every $1,000 per year income. If a family earns $5,000 per year, they give $5 per week through the church. If this formula were used by all families in every church there would be no financial problems. This amount, incidentally, works out to be one-half tithe.

Tithing is not the only measure for our giving to God through His Church.

I am opposed to tithing if it is used as a means of bargaining with God. This is the basis on which many church members promise to tithe. The formula becomes, "I will give you one-tenth. Just make sure I receive the other nine-tenths." As someone has written, "If we throw a loaf of bread on the waters then we expect a whole bakery to come floating back." As a further lever in their bargaining they quote Malachi 3:10. They hold it in God's face as if He had signed a promissory note.

Too much emphasis has been laid on this aspect of tithing. Some of the experiences are almost fantastic. One man said he struck oil almost every time he bored because he was in partnership with the Big Fellow and He made geology. A millionaire states he would never have been able to tithe his millions if he had not tithed his first salary which was $1.50 per week. An insurance executive states he tithed the first commission he collected and since then has lost very few prospects. A lawyer testified his income grew to almost $100,000 a year because he tithed his earnings from the very first. If this is the reason for tithing, then to my mind it is sacrilegious.

I am opposed to tithing if it is just another "gimmick" to get money. I am prompted at times to question the motives behind such promotions as thirteen weeks of tithing immediately prior to Easter or Christmas. On the surface we state it is a time when church people may experiment with tithing. We say that once they have witnessed the joy which comes from it, they will continue tithing. Underneath, however, where we face ourselves honestly, we must confess that in most instances it is just another way to get people to give more than they already give so the squeeze on the church treasury may be eased. We find this is just another trick to raise more money, and it is wrong.

IN FAVOR OF VOLUNTARY TITHING

Taking a more positive approach, I am in favor of tithing if the individual Christian sincerely believes he should tithe. This must be a personal decision. When a Christian discusses tithing, if he makes it a matter of reading and study, if he makes it a subject of deep concern in prayer, and, after all this, he is convinced he should tithe, then tithing is right for him. He will not be happy giving less. In this way, tithing becomes a spiritual rebirth.

I am in favor of tithing if it is recognized as a method of giving to God without pressure. To be sure, once we are convinced that tithing is for us, then we do not feel pressure because it becomes something we want to do—it then becomes a must. Consequently, if we can accept tithing freely, by inward motivation, without coercion from God or from man, tithing is good.

A boy was not getting his schoolwork. He would not do his assignments. He would not cooperate in his class and he was at odds with his teachers. He and his parents could not understand one another. With the passing of the months there was a noticeable change for the better. His work improved, his grades were higher, he became a leader in his class, his teachers were mystified and his parents were highly pleased. Why such a dramatic change: He had been motivated to realize his education was important. He decided he needed and wanted his schooling. He became aware, also, there was no pressure on him from the outside. All motivation was from within. If we can accept tithing in the same spirit, then I believe it is good.

Furthermore, I am for tithing if it is a means of bringing spiritual joy to the giver. This, it seems to me, is the paramount test of any religious practice. I am convinced that the individual, or family, practicing tithing finds a new joy in his

Christian life. Those who do not tithe find it difficult to understand what joy the tither has.

THE PROOF IS IN THE ACT

The joy of tithing is hard to understand until we have tithed. The non-tither says it cannot be done, he thinks of his many obligations, his plans for the future interfere, he is sure there is not enough to go around; so tithing is pronounced impractical and impossible. As sound as these objections may be, there is one thing about tithing of which I am convinced: Those who have been persuaded that tithing is for them and who practice it, find a new joy in their religious experience. If this is the result, I am for tithing!

I wish I could give credit for the following story which I heard many years ago. It was a thrilling story which has motivated me each time I think of it.

A young man, about 32, was earning a monthly salary of $300. He was married and had two small boys. He was paying rent, paying on an old car and trying to pay off a few doctor's and dentist's bills. On each pay day he gave his wife $20 for "house money" and deposited the rest in the checking account. He wrote out checks to pay the bills and usually ended up with nothing left. It was not unusual to borrow from his wife's house money before the next pay check was received.

At times he overdrew his checking account but was able to manipulate things so no checks were ever returned. He would influence a friend to hold a check until another check cleared. In this manner he kept a good credit rating but barely did so.

One Sunday morning something happened that was a turning point in his life, although at the time he thought he must be mentally breaking apart. The young man was in a Sunday school class taught by an elderly Christian gentleman who

gave himself to bringing others into an understanding of
Jesus as their Redeemer. On this particular Sunday, the
teacher had given an outstanding lesson on tithing. At the
close of the lesson, he asked how many men in the class were
tithers. Four of the men raised their hands but our young
subject was not among them. He rationalized that these men
were older, had their children raised, their houses paid for
and could easily tithe, but he was too financially strapped to
try it.

Then the teacher began to get rather personal. He asked
how many in the class would try tithing for a year? None.
How many would try for six months? None. Feeling he was
being repulsed, he pointed his finger directly at the young
man and asked him if he would not, as a personal favor to
the elderly teacher, try tithing for just three months. The
young man did not want to offend the older man so on the
spur of the moment and in the heat of embarrassment promised to do so.

When he had time to think it over, he wondered what in
the world he had done. He told his wife later in the day of
the promise he had made. She ungracefully told him they
could not do it and wondered how he could be so stupid as
to promise such a thing. He agreed with her but he had given
his word and would keep it.

Next pay day before he paid another bill, he laid aside the
tenth, gave his wife her house money, then set about to pay
the rest of the bills, or at least as many of them as possible.
The next Sunday he decided he would double the amount
he had been giving to the church. This made him feel good.

Each pay day he set aside the one-tenth. The amount in
the tithing jar was increasing. He was getting so much in the
jar that he was quite anxious for the three months to end so
he could grab the money and use it for other purposes. No
doubt his wife had visions of the same thing. Nevertheless,
he continued to put the amount aside and oddly enough

found he was no worse off financially than he had been before. There were still bills which had to be paid, no more than previously. The bank had stopped calling to tell him he was overdrawn.

One Sunday before the three months were up the Sunday school teacher met the young man in the corridor and told him three months were really not long enough for a trial at tithing. He influenced him to try another three months.

At the end of the six months, the young businessman went to his Sunday school teacher and told him he was going to continue to tithe. He had discovered a few things: He still had to pay the rent, and the doctor and the dentist, but the 90 percent left was going farther than the 100 percent earlier. He began to feel he was a bigger man within himself, his community and his church. He was contributing to community activities and taking a greater interest in them. He was giving 300 percent more to his church and assuming greater responsibility in it. He was learning how to take care of God's 10 percent and his own 90 percent much better. In this young man's life there had come a spiritual growth which far surpassed any material benefit he might have derived.

I am convinced that tithing is the most effective and most favorable method of financing church programs. However, it must be endorsed by the individual, on a very personal basis, to become a spiritual experience. It cannot be handed down by fiat.

To tithe or not to tithe! That is the question. True, it is the question, but it must be answered by the individual.

Chapter 3

CRUTCH-GIVING

IN A SUBURB of Philadephia, Pennsylvania, a clergyman was making pastoral calls. In hurrying from one call to the next, he accidentally bumped into another person. The minister apologized: "Please excuse me for my carelessness. I'm the pastor of Pinecrest Methodist Church up the street and was thinking of other things instead of watching where I was going."

The other person said: "I'm Mr. Wilson and I'm pleased to meet you. I've been supporting you and your church for some time." The minister was surprised, as he did not recognize the man, so he said: "I'm pleased to know that, but I don't recognize you as being in our congregation on Sunday mornings and I don't recall seeing your name on our church records."

Mr. Wilson replied: "I'm not a member of your church; in fact, I never attend your services. But, for the past number of years, each time your church has had a turkey dinner I bought tickets. My family attends these dinners and enjoys them." Here is a man who never attends a worship service in this church, nor is he a member of it. In fact, he is a complete stranger to the pastor and yet considers himself a supporter of the church.

A church which depends on this type of financial support

is open to the charge that it is a publicly supported organization. Pinecrest Methodist Church was dependent, largely, on the success of turkey dinners and such. In one sense this church was a public charge and the church budget was underwritten by the semblance of a community fund.

GIMMICKS IS CRUTCH-GIVING

For years the churches have depended on this and similar kinds of financial support for their programs. This kind of support has come not only from those who claim no association with the church, but from many within the church who believe this is the easiest and cheapest way to support the church. There is no doubt that there are many churches which have been saved from bankruptcy and many a minister and his family who have been saved from starvation because the main support has come in this manner.

The term I give for these methods is "gimmicks." However, as one studies this word and considers its roots, he may conclude it is a cruel and uncharitable word. "Gimmick" is defined as "anything artful or tricky; any cunning and secret device." I do not apologize for the use of the word "gimmicks" but I believe a more descriptive word is "crutch-giving."

The term "crutch-giving" was first brought to my attention by a devoted layman during an institute session of the Center for Church Business Management, The American University, Washington, D.C. When I began talking about gimmicks used by churches to support their budget, this layman explained that he called these things "crutch-giving." I have adopted this term because it seems more charitable and does not have quite the harsh overtones of "gimmick."

"Crutch-giving" describes quite adequately the kind of church financial support of which we speak in this chapter. Crutches are an artificial means of support which we use when we do not have sufficient strength to support ourselves.

The use of crutches indicates that something is wrong and we have to depend on a support beyond ourselves. Church giving which is motivated by something other than our own devotion and love of God can be called "crutch-giving."

The term "crutch-giving" may be new to many of us, but that to which it refers is not. Crutch-giving is not the result of inflation. Crutch-giving has been a weakness of the church from the time it began to be supported by voluntary gifts. In a country where there is a State, or established, church, the church is supported by taxation. This provides financial support but seems to create a spiritual problem.

The purpose of this chapter is to consider some of the practices of crutch-giving in our own country. For years the United States had a rural economy and citizens made everything for themselves. There was no manufacturing of merchandise for sale. Families were units of self-providers, and, consequently, when it came to support of the church and the clergy, gifts were made "in kind" rather than in money. The pastor was given a parcel of ground on which he built his own home, raised his own food and maintained his own stock. Support from his parishioners was in the form of food, livestock, some firewood and very little cash. The church was supported in the same manner: The parishioners supplied the building material and the man-hours to erect the church. They gave the firewood to heat the building in the winter and provided any maintenance that was necessary. A rural economy required this type of support.

VOLUNTARY CASH OFFERINGS INTRODUCED

The nation changed from a rural to an industrial economy and more cash became available to more people. Both the church and the clergy were affected by the change—they too needed cash.

Large towns and cities were becoming more populous. Denominations were meeting the challange of this population growth by establishing churches where the people were. Pastors were being assigned to these parishes, but there was no land available where they could grow their own food or keep livestock. Their parishioners, also, were involved in selling their time and their skill for cash payment, so they were no longer as independent as they once were. Gifts "in kind" were insufficient either to support the pastors or the churches. A new procedure of support had to be incorporated.

Church leaders began encouraging members to support the church through voluntary offerings in cash, but the results were discouraging. Wages were low, living conditions were poor, and extra money was scarce. It was much easier to bring in barrels of old clothes to be sent to the "heathen" across the sea than it was to give hard-earned cash. There appeared to be greater satisfaction in giving worn-out and discarded furniture to the pastor and his family than in giving a satisfactory salary so he could provide for himself. Parsonage families were called upon to make almost unbearable sacrifices. Many men left the ministry to better provide for their families. Those who had the courage to remain, lived in poverty and privation.

One of the early annual conferences of Methodism established the pastor's salary at $62 a year. The same amount was to be paid to his wife "if she needed it." For each child to age 6 the pastor received $15 a year, and for each child from 6 to 11 years old he received $20 a year. Only a few of these men received the allotted amount. Those who happened to get more than their allotment were to report it to the annual conference so it could be divided among the pastors who came up short.

Voluntary giving was not meeting expectations. This was true of every church that tried it. In order to make up the deficit, other schemes and methods had to be tried. Consequently, we come to the age of gimmicks or crutch-giving.

THIS IS WHAT HAPPENED

One of the first attempts at crutch-giving was that of sell-ing or renting church pews. In early church construction there were no seats; the congregation stood during the service. Eventually a pew was put in for the pastor's family —right down front. Then families of wealth, military officers and state officials began to request pews for their families. Space was set aside and the pews were constructed in boxlike form. Doors and locks were placed on these boxlike pews so none but the owners could sit in them. Some of these early church pews still exist in the colonial church edifices in our country.

As pews became more popular, they could be purchased outright or they could be rented. If rented, the rent was raised or lowered at the whim of the church officials. If, how-ever, the pews were personal property, the owner could sell them just as he would sell any other piece of property. It was not unusual to make a good margin of profit in the deal. The selling or renting of pews was a method of crutch-giving financing in the colonial church. The income was the finan-cial salvation of many congregations. However, the social jealousies and the spiritual evils overcame the benefits. Fam-ilies became jealous of each other because some had more prominent pews than others. There were those who were able to pay more and thus occupy the front pews, while others had to be satisfied to sit where it was difficult to see or hear or perhaps in the balcony with the servants. Such feelings disrupted the spiritual progress of the members in-dividually and of the church as a whole.

The practice of renting church pews still existed in the early 1900's in many city churches. The story is told that Mark Twain visited such a church one Sunday morning. He took the first available vacant pew. During the course of the service he received a note which stated, "You are sitting in our pew for which we pay $50 a year rent." Mark Twain sent back another note stating, "You are paying too much."

LOTTERIES

Another form of church financing was the lottery. Lotteries were commonplace. Whole communities used lotteries to finance community buildings; colleges used them to raise money for buildings and equipment, and the church endorsed lotteries. The prizes were always to be cash, and in some instances it took so long to raise the amount of money needed, the lotteries were never held. In other instances many thousands of dollars' worth of lottery tickets were sold in order to clear a few hundred dollars. In either case, the public was the loser.

Eventually, government officials became aware of the evils of lotteries and established laws forbidding them. After the conscience of the government had been aroused, the conscience of the church was aroused and church lotteries were banned. However, having discovered lotteries as a way to raise money with little effort and because a weakness of human nature is to get something for nothing, the old practice did not die but just changed colors.

For instance, an autographed picture of the First Lady of the land may be used as a prize in a church lottery to be given to some lucky ticket holder. Some churches ask for a donation for which they give a ticket which might be the lucky number on "that beautiful automobile sitting there."

Some years ago when my wife and I were traveling south from the Pocono Mountains in Pennsylvania, we saw a sign on the front law of a church building advertising the drawing for a 20-foot cabin cruiser. The cruiser was a prize in a church lottery.

On another occasion, I sat in a worship service where the

pastor announced to his congregation that as they left the service that morning there would be men standing at each of the doors selling tickets and that there would be a prize for the holder of the lucky number. The money, he reminded them, would be used for a good purpose.

In many communities the only organization permitted to operate bingo games, or facsimiles thereof, is the church. For other groups such games are illegal. I am not a puritan, but I do not believe the church can afford to jeopardize its position in any community by compromising with evil. If an act is wrong for some, then it is wrong for the church. Civic authorities should not be put in the position of having to talk out of two sides of their mouths. Communities should not have double standards. Lotteries are evil whether conducted by a church or anyone else. To say the end justifies the means is burying one's head in the sands to avoid seeing the moral consequences of our acts.

One woman told me she never gambled but did purchase lottery tickets sold by churches. She stated that she was not interested in the prize but did it to help the church. When I asked her if she would give to the church if no prize was involved, she had nothing to say.

OTHER MONEY GETTERS

Lotteries are only one method of crutch-giving. The gimmicks used are as varied as churches. Merchandising by churches has become so popular that in some instances churches are competitors of the grocery store, the variety store and the restaurant. A greater evil is that the church has a tax-free status, whereas the businessman must pay his share of taxes.

This is discrimination of the highest degree. If the church wants a separation from the State then let us be separated and not seek tax favors. We want police and fire protection for our property; we want good roads, water and sewers. These cost money and unless the church pays its fair share of the cost, someone else must make up the difference. Consequently, when a merchant must pay taxes to operate his business, while the church becomes one of his competitors without paying taxes, then the businessman is put in an unfair position. If a church wants to operate a restaurant, or hobby shop or variety store, then let it be honest and pay its fair share of merchandise taxes. If it has an entertainment for which there is an admission charge, let the church pay the taxes which are due and not skirt the responsibility by calling "admission" a "donation."

As an illustration of this church merchandising, a letter received by hundreds of churches began: "Success in raising money for your treasury depends on three things: Sell low-priced Christmas wrappings and decorations that everyone wants and can use. . . . Pay only for what you sell, after you have sold it, and return the rest. . . . Start your campaign early." Thus, the businessman who pays high rent, high taxes, high upkeep and satisfactory wages must compete with the church, which pays nothing. Ironically, we expect this same businessman to generously support the church. How un-Christian can we get?

Then, of course, there is the familiar and always-present church dinner. Everything needed is donated by members of the congregation; the ladies of the church prepare it, the men serve it and the children sell the tickets. It is for a "good purpose," we are told. However, the man who operates the restaurant for a living must meet this competition. In many instances, if he tried to prepare food in the same kind of unhealthy and unsanitary conditions as found in some church kitchens, he would be closed up tight. But because it is the church, the health officials walk down the other side of the street, the businessman says nothing for fear of reprisals and the church continues to be the profiteer. Where, oh where, is our Christian ethic?

Then comes the potpourri of merchandising in the bazaar. I suggest we incorporate another ecclesiastical season in the church year. It will be called the Season of the Bah-Zahr with the liturgical color gold. The season will begin the first week in October and continue to the first Sunday in Advent. During this time of the year churches receive more free publicity than during any other time. Each church tries to compete with the other church in novel ideas.

There are hat shows, horse shows, hair shows, fashion shows and innumerable other shows to encourage people to support the financial program of the church.

In one article in a metropolitan newspaper on the East Coast were these announcements from four separate churches: "There won't be any need to buy a plane ticket to visit famous Tivoli Gardens of Copenhagen on November 3. Residents can do this without leaving town if they visit the parish bazaar of the Friendly Church. The organizers have patterned their decorations after the 120-year-old gardens which have won a reputation as the most unusual and extravagant in Scandinavia. . . . There will be a delightfully decorated bistro, and 'Antique and Accent Arcade,' herb shop, summer holiday and gift table, food and bake counter, book stall, flower mart, children's play center and nursery, and an art gallery of original paintings, as well as Christmas cards and decorations."

Same article, another church: "There'll be a partridge in a pear tree at the annual bazaar of University Church. The organization's nature artists are offering espaliered trees which bear out the requirements of the gifts in the 'Twelve Days of Christmas.' They are also offering dried floral swags, winter bouquets, tree arrangements and wreaths as well as stalls of dried materials for 'do-it-yourself' shoppers."

Same article, another church: "A country store and gift shop will be featured at the fall festival and roast beef dinner being held by Riverview Church." Still another church:

"Chairs, tables, chests, cabinets, and bridge tables with matching upholstered gold chairs will be some of the items going at the Pink Elephant sale to benefit the Community Church on two coming weekends."

All this is done in the name of the church. Could it possibly be done in the name of Christ?

MILES AND MILES OF DOLLARS

Other forms of crutch-giving are the coin-folders, the mile of pennies, the mile of dimes, the mile of dollars and the mite box. These are justified by some because there is no buying or selling, just giving. But we ask how many give by these means because it is Christian stewardship or merely to satisfy their curiosity?

Tricky methods are used to promote these schemes. One minister laid dollars end to end for a mile along the road near his church. Of course, he had men of the church stationed along the route so others would not help themselves to the dollars. Stewardship or showmanship?

Another minister put a clothesline across the front of the nave of a church and told the congregation he wanted them to pin dollar bills on the clothesline during both the morning and evening worship hours. Following the morning worship service he took the clothesline, with the dollars on it, to his home for safekeeping. That evening it was quite a sight to see him bringing the line and the dollars back to the church. He looked like a snake charmer with line and dollars tangled around his body.

One of the most questionable, and perhaps most unethical, of the practices I have witnessed was at a meeting in Ohio. The pastor stood before the congregation holding in his hand a dollar bill which he had taken from his wallet. Holding it up so all could see he said, "I have a dollar bill, who has another one?" One of the men showed a dollar and the minister walked down to the man and exchanged dollars. The minister then showed that dollar and repeated the question. Another dollar was shown, so the minister traded those two. He continued to do this until the dollars had been exchanged several times. He asked everyone holding one of the bills to hold them high so they could be seen. When it appeared there were sixty or seventy dollars being shown, the pastor announced, "I do not know who has my dollar and I do not care what you do with it, but I am going to put this dollar I have in the offering plate." At that point the plates were passed and, of course, everyone did what the pastor expected they would do, put the dollars in the plates. Let us hang our heads in shame for such behavior and such carnival tricks done in the name of Christ!

The end is not yet! A congregation is encouraged to shop at a specific store, turn their sales slips into the church once a month and in turn the businessman will make cash settlement on a percentage basis with the church treasurer. Every congregation ought to rise up against such practices. The price of the merchandise may be higher, or the quality of the goods inferior, but since the church receives some benefit no one protests. The practice would soon disappear if members of congregations refused to do business on such terms.

One day while traveling through a town in Maryland, I came across another unusual gimmick for church fund raising. I passed a church building on which was a sign stating the church was sponsoring a bus trip to Atlantic City, New Jersey, the proceeds of which would be used for the church. On taking a closer look at the date for the trip I was surprised to note it was a Sunday. This meant that the congregation "closed shop" and went away for a day of fun and spending money in order to raise a little money for the church.

It seems the list of gimmicks, devices and crutch-giving is endless. What a disgrace to those who state a belief and faith in God. How belittling to have an outside observer call the church "an army that moves on its belly." We have the greatest news the world has ever heard! However, the greatest news which comes from some congregations is that they are having a supper, a bazaar, a fashion show, an art show or some other gimmick to finance their program. It is unfortunate that we must resort to tricks, gimmicks and questionable practices to get those who state that they love God and who claim the love of God for themselves, to give to that very cause which alone will save the world.

SOUL SEARCHING NEEDED

We need soul searching! A lack of financial support by members of a church may indicate that they have become more concerned about themselves than they are about the God whom they worship, the Christ in whose name they pray and the purposes for which a church exists. Self-centeredness blinds us to the needs of others. It makes us more aware of what we do not have rather than of what we have and it causes us to want more "unnecessities," more comforts, more gadgets, more conveniences, and it interferes with our doing for those who do without.

In order to compensate for self-centeredness we resort to crutch-giving and gimmicks which force us to support the church. When an offering plate is passed we may or may not put anything in; no one but ourselves, and God, knows what we have given, or if we have given. But when we are approached to buy a ticket for a dinner, or a lottery ticket or a fruit cake—if we do not respond then we are made to feel like freeloaders. Consequently, we support under compulsion; stewardship has been removed.

How much honor do we give our church when we support it under compulsion and especially when we must enlist the support of others, both friendly and unfriendly? Most of us feel a loss of dignity if we have to ask neighbors to help support our families, many would prefer to live in privation than suffer such humility; yet, we are not averse to the solicitation of support from anyone who will help keep our churches from financial embarrassment.

We proclaim the doctrines of truth, honesty and integrity; therefore, we must uphold the law and not seek favors from civic officials by asking them to close their eyes or turn their backs while we participate in questionable practices and in some instances engage in out-and-out lawbreaking. Let the church come forward and willingly pay taxes on income, property and amusements, rather than use devious procedures to avoid taxes.

Above all, and this is last because it is most important, let us be motivated by our love and devotion to Almighty God. If we put Him and His Son, Jesus, in the place they should be in our lives, right in the center, many of these gimmicks and the need for crutch-giving would soon pass away.

Throw open the doors of our lives to the influence of the Holy Spirit and let His power consume us. We will be so motivated that we will give ourselves and all we have to God through His Church. The crutches can be thrown away and we will walk free again. It was said of the Macedonians, "First they gave themselves to the Lord."

We need to do away with our crutch-giving and our gimmicks to get down to the roots of genuine giving. Genuine giving has in it several qualities which the Christian church needs to grasp again. Much of our evangelistic fervor has been lost because we have been too concerned about getting money to keep the doors open rather than being concerned about the souls of our fellowmen through the burning of the Holy Spirit on our altars.

Genuine giving has in it a self-sacrificing quality. The Macedonians mentioned above could not afford to give what they gave. They gave out of their poverty. It could not have been much that was given, but the important thing was that they gave.

Sacrificial giving is a basic ingredient to genuine giving. Some years ago I had an experience in Canada that pointed up the truth of this statement. A small church needed a new building for worship and they made an intensive drive for funds. On the Sunday the actual canvass began, the pastor announced to the congregation that he believed in what was being done and he and his family were giving liberally to it. At the close of the service one of the laymen, who was earning much more than his pastor but was giving one-third less, told me he believed his pastor was giving too much. He said, "He cannot afford to give that amount." That was true! He could not afford to give what he gave, but because he did, it was genuine giving.

St. Paul makes an interesting statement about contrasting states of circumstances: He said the Macedonians had abundant joy and extreme poverty. This is almost beyond comprehension to us as we have come to feel that poverty and sadness go hand in hand, while wealth and joy are constant companions. This is not the case, for many people who live with practically nothing are among the happiest.

In our soul searching about genuine giving, we discover another component is spontaneity. There is no need for someone to compel, to coax or to pressure us into purchasing something so the church may make a small profit. Spontaneity in our giving results from that which is within and does not come about because of some pressure from outside. "Free will" is a synonym for "spontaneous," and "spontaneous" implies an uninhibited, unrestrained response rising deep from within the individual.

It is significant to note that we can always find a way to do what we want to do without any pressure from those around us. A mother does not have to be forced to love her children. A father does not have to be compelled to show devotion and kindness to his offspring and we do not have to be forced to give our support to the church by devious and tricky devices if we have a deep love for God and His Kingdom. We will always find a way to do the thing we want to do—including support to our church.

Another component in genuine giving is earnestness, enthusiasm or zeal. The need for crutch-giving is aroused because we have lost something of the warmth and zeal for our religion. There is a great difference between the crutch-giver and the individual who burns with a desire to be a part of an on-going program and gives himself and all he has to it.

In our giving, we need something of the same enthusiasm of the elderly woman who gave expression to her feeling in the worship service by shouting words of praise. Whenever the minister said something with which she agreed, she made it known by shouting "Praise God!" However, this annoyed the pastor, so he requested his officials to talk to her about it. She promised she would be quiet and lived up to her promise for a while. One Sunday she was carried away with emotion and let her feeling be known. The pastor decided he would try to get her to be still. He promised he would give her two expensive blankets if only she would not disturb him in the services by her shouting. This sounded good to the elderly woman, and she made her promise. For weeks nothing was heard from her. Then one Sunday morning the pastor waxed strong on some subject. The elderly woman squirmed in her seat, doing her best to keep quiet. When she could endure it no longer, she stood up and shouted, "Blankets or no blankets, praise God!" This inner motivation, this enthusiasm in our giving will help us to do away with gimmicks and all crutch-giving.

The final component of genuine giving is in first giving ourselves to God. The greatest measure of our giving is based on our love of God and of Him alone. We are not entirely motivated by our devotion to the church—as important as that is. We are not motivated wholly by the kind of program our church presents to the community and the world. It is not what we like or dislike about the church and the congregation: Our giving is based on our love of God. When we have given ourselves, when we have laid our families on the altar in devotion to God, when we have held nothing back in the way of material and physical contributions, then our giving will be sacrificial, spontaneous, enthusiastic and deeply motivated. There will be no need of gimmicks, crutches or any other superficial prompting to support the church.

Let us throw away the crutches and walk uprightly by faith in God!

PLEDGE? WHO, ME?

AN INNOVATION in the early American church was voluntary support. Most colonists had come from countries where the church was financed by taxation. Now they were in a new country where the pressure of religious legalism had been eased. They found it difficult to wean themselves from some of their old practices. They had freedom but did not know what to do with it. Voluntary support for the churches was one of the most difficult new ideas in their freedom to adopt.

There was no compulsion to support the church. The settlers were free to return to the principle of the church in Apostolic days when St. Paul asked for a collection of money from Christians in Corinth for the relief of Christians in Jerusalem. Each individual determined for himself what he would give.

It must be noted that this freedom in voluntary giving did not prevail everywhere in this new country. There were communities under the domination of landlords or of the Church of England. Assessments were common and taxes were raised for church support. However, for many people, the new-found political freedom meant freedom, also, in supporting the church.

Unfortunately, voluntaryism was not successful. Churches

suffered financial embarrassment, mission programs were unknown, ministers and their families suffered privation. To overcome this financial dilemma, methods were innovated to raise money for the church. Some of these are discussed in the preceding chapter.

FATHER OF THE PLEDGE

One of these methods which received acceptance was the "subscription list." This was a list on which the members indicated their gift to support the pastor and the church. The gifts were in kind and not in cash. Donations for the pastor were firewood, salt, whiskey, linen, flour, tobacco and meat, among other things; gifts for the church were lumber, nails, man-hours and animal-hours. Once one wrote his name, or just initials, his subscription was binding. The law stated that the subscription had to be made good.

The subscription list was the forerunner of the pledge card system used today. The purpose of this chapter is to discuss the use of pledges in the church financial structure.

Because of frequent opposition to the word "pledge," we suggest several other words. To pledge connotes legalism and frequently it is interpreted in terms of a binding contract. Many are reluctant to sign a pledge card because they believe they are legally bound to the terms of the card. One alternative is the word "subscription." Overtones of legalism are subdued. Willing assent is predominant. There is inference of agreement with the program. For instance, when one says, "I subscribe to that doctrine," he is really saying, "I believe in it and will support it." We subscribe to a financial program because we believe in it and will support it.

Another alternate word is "commitment." Commitment is more encompassing and has deeper meaning than either pledge or subscription. To commit one's self is more than promising to do something, as in the pledge, and it is more than being in agreement with an idea. To commit one's self implies more than financial support. It is giving one's whole self, everything, to God through the church. Commitment is synonymous with stewardship.

One other alternate word is "estimate." Webster states that an estimate is "a value determined by judgment, where exactness is not sought or is not attainable." In a church financial program, an estimate indicates what a donor desires to give but is unable to commit himself to with exactness. "Estimate" allows freedom and change. I think the Congregational Christian Church comes nearest to this idea by naming their cards "Declaration of Intention."

These alternates for the word "pledge" are suggested because there is a form of magic in the right use of words. To speak of an "estimate card" or "commitment card" or "subscription card" will frequently break down resistance of obstinate members who will completely ignore a pledge card. Regardless of which term is used, however, the goal is always the same: to have members of the church underwrite the church budget.

As stated above, the pledge card system is the offspring of the subscription list. The difference is that instead of a list being circulated for every family or member to sign, an individual card is distributed, thus affording some secrecy regarding the amount given. For the sake of simplicity the term "pledge" will be used in this chapter.

NONAGREEMENT

There is a diversity of opinion regarding the use of pledges, not only among denominations but within denominations. For instance, the Methodist denomination encourages an annual every-member canvass in each church. The emphasis is on participation by each member who signs a pledge card. Excellent promotional material is made available free or at minimum cost. Workshops and retreats are conducted to train local church leaders in setting up canvasses. High level denominational leaders travel throughout the country speaking about and promoting these every-member visitations. The whole power of the Methodist denomination is behind the program. In spite of all this effort, many Methodist churches have never used pledge cards in their membership and continue to resist their use.

The following is typical of such churches. In Ohio, there is a rural Methodist church whose members staunchly object both to a church budget and to pledging. These people support their church, but they will make no financial forecast either in needs or in expectations. The pastor is paid regularly. When the time comes to meet denominational apportionments, the pastor announces how much is needed and the people give. If the furnace breaks down or the roof leaks or the building needs painting, the pastor gets estimates of the respective costs and on the following Sunday announces how much money is needed and the people give. Let it be emphasized: They give—liberally! These people have money, they will not permit their church to suffer because of lack of finances, but let the pastor ask this congregation to make a pledge or to formulate a budget and he has a revolt on his hands.

Some years ago I worshiped in a church in Scranton, Pennsylvania. It was an evening service at which several hundred people were in attendance. At the appointed time the pastor announced that the offering would be received. Offering plates were passed and taken to the front of the nave. Then, much to my surprise, the men who had received the offering sat down at a table where all could see them and began to count how much they had received. The pastor in the meantime continued with the service. After some time, one of the men stood up, stopped the pastor in what he was doing and whispered to him. The pastor announced immediately that another offering was to be received because not enough had been given the first time around. So the plates were passed the second time. This procedure was repeated, the money was counted, one of the men later whispered something to the pastor, who again announced that another offering was to be taken. This time they apparently got what they needed, because we were not asked for any more money that night. This is an extreme case, to be sure, but it can happen unless there is wise planning.

Churches of many denominations operate each year without a formal budget and without pledges. In fact, some pastors of these denominations consider budgets and pledges as a work of the devil which undermines the individual's privacy and interferes with his devotion to God. Conversely, I have talked to other ministers in these same denominations who wish the pledge system could be initiated among their people.

One minister in a denomination that looks with disfavor on both budgets and pledges told me his whole church program suffers because of this attitude. He had approximately three hundred members in his church. None of them committed themselves to any set amount toward the church budget and their level of giving was low. The missionary program compared favorably with other churches in his denomination, but he was ashamed of how little was being done in the total denominational program. The local church property was kept in good repair, but little was done to advance the educational work or the music program. The pastor and his family were called on to make many sacrifices because he was inadequately compensated. It was his feeling that many of these problems would have been solved if an annual budget were formulated and pledges were made to support it.

It is my opinion there should be an annual budget in every church. It shows that the church officials know the direction in which they are going. There is order instead of chaos, direction instead of wandering, thought instead of chance. After the budget has been formulated, then the congregation should be motivated to support it by pledges through a love of God and not just for the sake of making a pledge.

PRE-BUDGET OR POST-BUDGET CANVASSES

There are two schools of thought on when pledges should be made for the church budget. There are those who advocate that the congregation make pledges first and, after the results are in, the committee on finance will formulate the budget on the basis of the pledges. Others state the budget should be determined first and then be submitted to the congregation for their support.

Proponents of the first school argue that the church is on a firmer foundation if the people state what they will give before the budget is made up. Adherents of the second method insist it is a greater challenge to the congregation if the goals of the church are established first.

Dr. David R. Holt, II, in *Handbook of Church Finance*, refers to these procedures as the pre-budget and the post-budget canvass systems. It is his feeling that in the pre-budget system a church gets a more accurate idea of what the members will give, that it is a higher view of stewardship, and there is better motivation in giving. In the post-budget system he maintains that people are more inclined to give to the budget rather than to God through His church.

I favor post-budget canvasses. The spiritual tone of such a canvass is as high and meaningful as in pre-budget canvasses. I have witnessed post-budget canvasses bring about a deep spiritual reawakening in a congregation. The after-effect has been as forceful as a revival. Such a spiritual result depends on the orientation and training both of the congregation and the canvassers. Emphasis is placed on the need of the giver to give for his own spiritual growth. He is made aware that his gift is not in money to the church, but it is the giving of himself and all he possesses to God. Spiritual motivation is the first requirement in a canvass.

I favor post-budget canvasses because a goal is held before the congregation. There is a tendency in all of us to maintain the status quo in almost everything we do. This tendency is manifested in our giving to the church. If left to our own feelings, therefore, most of us would give the same amount year after year. However, when a goal has been set before a congregation in the form of a budget, then each member must restudy his giving in the light of the total needs. A church program cannot become static. There must be forward movement. In the same sense, the church member cannot become static in his support of the church program. Each year there should be some increase in the church budget, regardless how small, so each member will feel the need to increase his financial participation.

I favor post-budget canvasses because the church program is stronger when the needs are studied beforehand. When the various committees and commissions seriously study their financial needs for a coming year, they are at the same time projecting themselves into the future program of the church. They envision their goals and set projects for themselves. Such study strengthens the overall progress of the church and makes for a dynamic program. This, to my mind, is much better than waiting to see how much a congregation is willing to give and then telling the various groups to go out and do their best with what is available to them.

ARE PLEDGES LEGAL?

In returning to the question: How legal is the pledge, it should be pointed out that under certain circumstances the pledge has been found to be a legally binding contract and is, therefore, enforceable. However, before any final conclusions are drawn, especially by those who may use this as an excuse for not pledging, further explanation must be given. The usual pledge card is not a binding contract, the wording used determines its legal or nonlegal status. For instance, if the card states, "Remembering my vows to be loyal to my church by attendance, prayers, gifts and services, I will undertake to support the church financially for the church program $20 per week," or if it merely states, "We hereby pledge to the Springfield Methodist Church $20 per week for the church program": neither of these forms is legally binding.

In order to further remove any fear from the donor, it is suggested this sentence be placed at the bottom of the card: "This pledge may be revised or cancelled at the request of the donor at any time." This statement tells the donor he is free to lower his pledge, to raise his pledge or to cancel his pledge. Further, this statement releases him from any legal action possibly contemplated. All that is necessary is for the donor to place a telephone call to the proper official in the church and make his request; there is no embarrassment.

However, if the card states, "In consideration of the gifts of others, we hereby pledge $20 a week to the Springfield Methodist Church for the church program," this may be declared binding. It has been ruled that the phrase "In consideration of" is sufficient to put the card in the category of a legal contract and may, therefore, be enforced. Let those responsible for printing pledge cards make certain there is nothing legally binding. The church is for the purpose of making life free of anxiety, not adding burdens to it.

The idea of legal enforcement of pledges causes a shudder to go through me. In Washington, D.C., a religious group took one of its members into court, charging he had promised to make a substantial donation to his group. On the basis of his statement, the congregation proceeded to install a decorative room in their building. A large outlay of money was required. Several years passed but no payment on the pledge had been made. The congregation brought suit to collect for the large amount of money they had spent unnecessarily. I talked to a member of the congregation about the court action. He was quite embarrassed about it and felt that there were mitigating circumstances causing the donor not to pay, that there had been some misunderstandings in communication and that the newspaper reports were not giving the whole picture.

I cannot conceive of church officials taking a member of a church to court to force payment of a pledge. It seems to me that before any church brings suit against an individual or a family for nonpayment of a pledge, sincere investigation should be made by someone in the church to determine why the pledge had not been paid. I believe such investigation would provide sufficient evidence to show that the family was in need of spiritual or material help from their fellow members of the church. Instead of dragging them into court, it would be more advisable to lift them into the presence of God through our interest and our prayers.

In one church a family with three children were staunch financial supporters of the church. Their envelopes were brought in each Sunday and their pledge was always current. Then it was noted they were getting in arrears and were giving irregularly. This was brought to the attention of the pastor. He called on the family, not to talk about finances, but to inquire about their general welfare. He learned that one of the children had been found mentally inadequate. Professional service for the child became a heavy drain on the family finances. At the same time he learned that the father had suffered a setback in income and this added further to the family's problems. The pastor was told the family had continued giving to the church even after cutting back on other obligations. However, they were finally forced to make some adjustment in their giving to the church. The pastor was quite sympathetic. He made known the plight of the family to several others in the church. Instead of taking the family into court to make good on their pledge, their fellow members in the church came to their support by offering financial assistance.

EXCUSES FOR NOT PLEDGING

All excuses for not making a pledge should be recognized as symptoms of disinterest in the program, spiritual immaturity and/or incorrect solicitation. It is right that members of a church should make sacrificial pledges to their church. It is wrong that Christian families should deny their church their full support and deny themselves the spiritual experience of generous pledging to their church.

On the other hand, it must be acknowledged that giving is a habit, and most church members cultivate a weak habit in this regard. We enjoy doing most what we do well. Many church members have been doing such a bad job of giving, they secure no enjoyment or satisfaction from it during their lifetime in any manner whatsoever. Therefore, excuses should not mislead church officials. Excuses may be offered in good faith so far as the prospect's conscious mind is concerned, but they are not the real reasons for saying no. They are indications that an inner struggle is in progress.

Excuses must be answered, but answers alone will not bring a person to a right decision. The following common excuses and answers may be of some help, but they are not the final word by any means.

One excuse is "I do not believe in pledging." It is important to note the pledge is more important than the gift. The matter of pledging one's self is at the very center of Jesus' teaching. True Christianity without pledging is impossible. On a purely commercial level, our entire business civilization is founded on the pledge. We pledge ourselves financially every day. If we bought or used only what we paid for in advance, we would have very little materially. On a purely selfish level, consider that we will pledge for anything we want badly enough: a home, a car, a refrigerator, a boat. At the same time, if we want a real spiritual existence for ouselves, we will pledge ourselves for it.

Another excuse is "I do not like something about the church." An excuse of this kind is usually a device whereby the member is unconsciously trying to get the church on the defensive, in this manner taking attention from his own errors of omission. An approach to make to one who offers this excuse is to try to persuade him to pledge substantially and to begin getting active in the church to see what is being done with his money. Once he has begun to work in the church, he can help correct what he does not like in it. No doubt his whole perspective will change.

Another excuse is "I do not want to be bound to something I am not sure I can fulfill." This casts a reflection on other members of the church. It is as if the member said, "I will not obligate myself because if something happens so I cannot pay what I have promised there will be no mercy and I will be forced to pay. To save embarrassment I will make no pledge. I will give what I can when I attend." This indicates a spiritual weakness. It reveals the donor will be erratic in giving and irregular in attendance.

Others make this excuse, "I want to wait and see how the canvass comes out." Frequently this is said by members who are in a position to make a substantial pledge. They imply, "If you do not get your goal I will make up the difference." This is not always the case. Actually, if they are among those who can make a large pledge they should be encouraged to do so. People are influenced by their financial superiors and have a tendency to follow their advice. It is the responsibility of financial leaders to lead financially and to make their support of the budget known so the membership will be encouraged to follow their example. To do otherwise is for the financial leaders to surrender their leadership responsibilities to the smaller givers and eventually to contribute to the failure of the budget canvass.

Excuses must be studied carefully. They may be nothing more than a protection of the pocketbook.

Before leaving this section on excuses, note that there are those in every church who make a pledge but who apparently have little or no intention of paying. They will not offer excuses and they sign willingly, frequently for a substantial weekly amount. It is difficult to understand why some members will do this year after year. It does happen, however, and there are so many who make a practice of this that officials in charge of church finances now discount percentages of the pledges knowing they will never be paid.

ATTAIN BROADER BASE OF GIVING

One desired result of pledging is to attain a broader base of giving. Frequently congregations depend on a few to give much. There are many who give little and there are some who give nothing. For instance, I know of a church of 750 family units. Of these, 482 families pledged, 268 made no pledge. Of the former there were a few who contributed through the weekly envelopes without pledging. The breakdown was:

   16 units gave less than $1
  176 units gave from $1 to $3
  142 units gave from $3 to $5
   80 units gave from $5 to $7
   32 units gave from $7 to $10
   35 units gave from $10 to $22
    1 unit gave $25

In this church about 5 percent of the congregation supported 18 percent of the subscribed budget. This ratio is not as glaring as it is in some churches. There are instances where 5 percent of the members are supporting 35 percent of the budget. Nevertheless, in any situation where the differential between the number of givers and the amount given is too great, there is a need for greater participation by the members.

To have 100 percent participation in pledging spreads the base of giving. If a church is to have a successful all-around program, including benevolences, then it is essential for every family in the church to make a pledge and to make every effort to pay in full.

To attain greater participation in pledging and giving indicates that the members are growing spiritually. By neglecting the financial aspect of our church affiliation, we deprive our soul of full development. Giving our possessions is as imperative for a complete Christian life as is praying. When a church allows its members to ride free on the "gospel train," that church is as negligent in its duties as if it neglected to help one of its members who is faltering in his spiritual life through dishonesty.

Furthermore, those who make a pledge to their church and carry through with it are most likely to develop into regular church attendants. It is a well-known fact that most pledges are paid weekly or biweekly, usually during the worship services, thus encouraging regular attendance.

IS WEEKLY OFFERING OBSOLETE?

There are some questions which need to be considered pertaining to the weekly offering. Is the weekly offering the best way to receive money for the church? Should other ways be devised to make it more convenient for people to remit their offerings to the church and at the same time let the church administrators know there will be a regular income?

Some steps are being taken in this area. For instance, there is a growing tendency to eliminate the weekly offering envelope. One reason is that many people are paid every two weeks or bimonthly. In turn they give to the church on the

same basis. Thus, some church officials believe it is more
economical to purchase biweekly, rather than weekly, envelopes. A large Methodist church in Nashville, Tennessee,
uses biweekly envelopes and attests to its success with their
congregation.

THE BANK ORDER

Another growing practice is for members of the congregation to give authority to their banks to pay to their church

---

Name _____

_____

Bank _____
Remembering God's goodness to me, and my vow to support the
Church according to my ability I Cheerfully promise to contribute
the indicated amount beginning_____ , 19__,
and continuing until further notice.
To: _____

WEEKLY	$20	$15	$10	$7	$5	$4	$3	$2.50	$2	$1.50	$1	75c	50c

MONTHLY: $_____   ANNUALLY: $_____
(This voluntary pledging may be changed or cancelled at any time by
notifying the Secretary.)
(Use 50 cents of my gift for subscription to "Trinity News.")

---

a stated sum at prearranged intervals—these are bank orders.
The financial secretary presents the bank orders on Monday
morning and credit is given to the church account; with-
drawals are automatic from the member's account. This use
of the bank order is extraordinarily successful in a Methodist
church in Tallahassee, Florida. Whenever the idea is first
presented to minister and laymen, there is great resistance.
But once the plan is understood and serious study given to it,
the resistance diminishes.

BANK ORDER

Your Town, U. S. A. _____ 19 _____

This is authority for THE PEOPLES BANK OF YOUR TOWN

Your Town, U. S. A.   to charge my account; $ _____
Monthly for the account of _____

beginning _____ , 19__, and continuing until
further notice.

_____

Authorized Signature

At the time the member makes his pledge to the church, he signs the authority for his church to present the bank orders against his account. This authority is continued until negated by the member. The members who use the system are so well pleased with it they do not want to use any other system. It avoids any embarrassment of arrearages during the year, because the bank order is presented weekly and the pledge is kept current. A most astonishing fact is that there is a 99 percent rate of collection with this system.

Proper care must be made in handling the bank order so the members will continue their confidence in the system. Extreme accuracy is required.

This system eliminates periods of poverty and periods of plenty in church income. The bank orders are year-round, so income is as great during the off-season as it is during the busy season of the church year. The church saves on postage since statements are mailed only twice a year.

This is a unique procedure in church fund raising and is well worth serious consideration by church administrators.

```
:BIT _____    $

    Received of THE PEOPLES BANK OF YOUR TOWN,  the amount stated hereon
  the account of _____ as per order now on file with this bank.

                        _____ , Treasurer

    Your Town, U.S.A._____ , 19_____    By _____

              Bank Account Number _____
```

MEMBERSHIP DUES

Another method meeting with success in some churches is to assess dues on the membership. Before one unites with the church he is informed of the needs of the church and what is expected from each member if the church is to be successful in its plans. If he does not wish to accept the responsibility, he may refuse to unite with the church. Once he has become a member, however, he is expected to pay his dues regularly and promptly. If he falls in arrears, a friendly reminder is sent to him. If he continues to remain in arrears and makes no effort to notify the proper officers why he is in arrears, then he is visited by someone trained to make a tactful call. If there is still no effort to become current, then a final notice is sent and in a given time the member is dismissed.

I know this procedure will receive severe criticism, but it is difficult to argue with success, and where the dues system is practiced, and the constituency notified of the method in advance, it is successful. One wonders if such a procedure would not raise the prestige of church membership. The church is the easiest and the cheapest fellowship to join. I have doubts about the "dues" policy, but it is worth considering and could ease the burden of church financing.

WHAT HAPPENS TO LITURGY?

There are questions! If church members remit their money in bank orders, or by forwarding checks through the mail to pay dues, or by returning a perforated card to be run through an electronic machine indicating payment of their pledge, what happens to the "Presentation of Tithes and Offerings" in the worship service? Would the symbolism of this part of the service be lost? Or would this act of worship be eliminated completely? The answer is No to both questions. There will always be those who give during the worship service and there will always be those who do not wish to cooperate in these new methods.

In fact, there are many worshipers who now go through the liturgical act of presenting an offering but who, in reality, have given their financial support through other means.

When I first learned of these new methods, they left me cold. They seemed empty of any spiritual significance. However, as the banking industry becomes more efficient in handling checks and other forms of exchange, as more people handle less cash because of better banking facilities, as we make more use of credit cards, it may be necessary for the whole complex of church finance to change in the next 25 years, just as it has changed over the past 25 years.

HOW SOON SHOULD NEW MEMBERS PLEDGE?

There is one other matter which merits attention: How soon after uniting with the church should new members be asked to pledge? There are at least four procedures. First, before the person is received into the church, members of the finance committee call on him and explain the financial program of the church. The prospective member is encouraged to ask questions. He is told the present range of giving and the anticipated standard of giving if the church is to be successful. The prospective member submits his pledge on the Sunday he unites with the church.

In a large church in Washington, D.C., the pastor meets with all who plan to unite with the church. One of the main emphases made during this meeting is the financial needs of the church. After making the presentation, the pastor hands out pledge cards and asks the members to commit themselves right then. When they are received into the fellowship of that church the pastor announces that each of the new members has already made his pledge to support the church financially.

Second, on the day he unites with the church, the new member is given a membership packet including offering envelopes, a pledge card, a copy of the church budget and other information. Enclosed, also, is a self-addressed envelope in which he may return his pledge to the church within the next ten days or two weeks. If no reply is received in that time, a member of the finance committee visits the new member to determine whether he has any questions about the church budget, to explain it in detail if necessary and to make every effort to get the signed pledge card with that visit.

Third, a few weeks go by before the new member is contacted about his pledge. He is given time to become acquainted with church goals, with other members and with the idea of his belonging. After several weeks someone calls at the member's home, explains the church budget, answers questions, leaves envelopes and makes every effort to get a pledge. If this fails, he asks that the card be brought to the church the following Sunday. This is not recommended as general procedure. Follow up if necessary.

The fourth method is tragic and should be discouraged. In this a new member is received into the church but nothing is said about the church budget. It is hoped he will become aware of the financial needs, will submit a pledge and will eventually give. The majority of those who unite know the church does not run on air or water. It must have money. They expect to contribute; however, if no one approaches the new member to explain the program, or no contact is made until the every-member canvass, which may be six or eight months later, then the potential of the new member may be lost. Most people are enthusiastic about their membership in a church when they first affiliate. To ignore them, or make them feel they are not needed or that the church can get along without them, is tragic!

Each church will determine for itself which method, or combination of methods, it will use.

ONLY ONE APPEAL

If pledges are asked to support the church budget there should be one, and only one, general appeal made during the year. All of the church's obligations and goals should be incorporated into that appeal. It shows lack of faith on the part of the church officials and is unfair to the congregation to encourage them to fully support the budget and then to make appeals for special contributions during the year. Encourage the congregation to underwrite the budget with the promise that no further efforts will be made, then stick to that promise!

This does not mean that stewardship of money will be forgotten during the rest of the year. There should be sermons, items in the newsletter and blurbs in the bulletin to lift up stewardship. It means that no begging and appealing and coaxing will be done during the worship services each Sunday during the year.

Pledge? Why not? "Remembering my vows to be loyal to my church by attendance, prayers, tithes and services, I will undertake to support the church financially."

To pledge or not to pledge—
  That is the question.
Whether 'tis nobler in a man
  To take the Gospel free
  And let another foot the bill,
Or sign a pledge and pay toward
  Church expense!
To give, to pay—aye, there's the rub,
  To pay—
When on the free-pew plan a man
  May have
A sitting free and take the Gospel, too,
  As though he paid, and none be ought
  The wiser
Save the church committee who—
  Most honorable men—can keep a secret!
"To err is human," and human, too, to buy
  At cheapest rate. I'll take the Gospel so!
For others do the same—a common rule!
I'm wise; I'll wait, not work—
  I'll pray, not pay,
And let the other fellow foot the bills,
And so I'll get the Gospel free,
  You see!

(Author Unknown)

Chapter 5

DEFERRED GIVING:
A NEW DIMENSION

THERE is now emerging among Protestant churches a new development in stewardship expression. It is one which, in the opinion of this observer, holds great promise for the Christian church of the next generation. This development is already under way; it will gather momentum in the next three to five years; significant fruitage from it will be apparent within twenty years.

A BASIC PREMISE

The development to which I refer is the increasing willingness of church members to bear witness to their Christian faith by arranging financial support for the church's work in these ways:

(1) bequests under will;
(2) lifetime transfers of capital sums under various plans, but notably under gift annuity agreement;
(3) giving of property in other forms than cash, typically negotiable securities;
(4) arranging benefits for church and charity through life insurance;
(5) setting up memorial or endowment-type gifts.

78

A characteristic of this kind of giving, almost without exception, is that the contributed amount is not intended for immediate use but is intended rather for use at some predetermined future time. Even though the transfer is irrevocable, and even though the prospect of its ultimate availability is assured, stipulated conditions must usually be fulfilled before sums so contributed may be used. To contrast gifts of this character with giving for current objectives, these typically are spoken of as "deferred gifts."

The giving procedures just set forth may seem to suggest implications that are mainly practical, technical or legal. Admittedly such elements are involved. Basic to all of them, however, are considerations that are profoundly spiritual. What we are concerned with, it seems to me, is something more than fund raising.

Involved is a new dimension in Christian stewardship. It is a dimension already experienced by some, but not yet ventured into by many. In proportion, as they advance their stewardship understanding to include it, the churches will be equipped for the opportunities for Christ that lie ahead.

Most Christians have, I think, a degree of understanding about "Christian calling." We recognize that God calls all men, that His own hear His voice and seek to respond to it. Response on the part of young people may take the form of affiliating with a congregation—for the sake of their children, perhaps, but also for the joys of participating in the Christian fellowship. At times it may take the form of accepting the chairmanship of a key committee, of being named Sunday school superintendent or of service in some other special way. We've all been mindful of a sense of call in instances like these.

Not so readily grasped, however, is the concept that God's call is a continuing one, extending over all of life's span. God's call isn't something to be experienced only by youth or by adults in the full vigor of life! God's call comes again and

again—to every believer, and in whatever situation of life
he or she happens to be. It is only the response that changes
its nature, its manner, its method, but not the call.

A spiritual insight not yet caught by most church members
is the realization that in the evening years of life—when the
demands and pressures of the earlier years are past—there
may be opportunities to witness to one's faith in ways that
simply weren't possible earlier.

A definition of call that I like is this: "A need recognized
and a capacity to meet that need for Christians constitutes
a call." There is no shortage of Christian causes or enterprises
that can use more support than they are getting. Deferred
giving may well be the means through which many in the
future achieve a sense of response previously beyond them.

An emerging development within church bodies gives
practical support to my conviction in this regard. Within one
month it was my privilege to counsel with representatives of
three church bodies, all of which were considering establishing, within their respective structures, agencies comparable
to the one with which I am associated. I know that at least as
many other churches within the past three years have already
instituted such agencies.

Called by many names—special gifts departments, foundations, offices of development—their function is the same: providing additional support for the church's work by bringing
members to deeper understanding of the church's mission
and to a level of stewardship commitment that finds expression in new ways of giving.

More is involved in this development, it seems to me, than
"keeping up with the Joneses." Someone once said, "Nothing
is so powerful as an idea whose time has come." I believe
that's what is being evidenced about us. A new dimension in
Christian stewardship is in process of development all across
the church!

To summarize, my thesis for this chapter is that in the

mature understanding of Christian vocation is indicated both the *premise* and the *strategy* for achieving what may be properly described as a new dimension in stewardship understanding and commitment. The fruitage of that dimension will be new strength for Christian enterprises everywhere and joyous fulfillment for those contributing to it.

Forward then to those specific things which pastors, lay leaders of congregations and specially appointed personnel can do to bring this hoped-for development to reality within your own fellowship!

A PROGRAM FOR ACTION

A program for development of deferred giving, either at the local level or within a denominational constituency, should seek to do these things:

(1) Set in motion among the members a long-term, low-pressure *educational* program on the subject of wills, bequests and estate planning. First emphasis of the program should be on the practical and spiritual importance of every adult church member having a will. Secondary emphasis should be on the several causes and aspects of the church's work which are basic to its mission and for which bequests of whatever amount might worthily be directed.

(2) Provide opportunity for members, able and willing to do so, to make contributions *while living* for those same purposes through such attractively modern plans as gift annuity agreement, life income agreement (both regular and tax-free) and through agreements of trust tailored to the individual situation.

(3) Remind members of the opportunities for creative giving afforded through life insurance and endowment policies.

(4) Recognize that some members may more conveniently make their contributions in some form other than cash, notably in the form of securities, and be prepared to receive them.

(5) Offer opportunity for members to capitalize their cur-

rent giving, or to otherwise extend their Christian influence, through the establishment of memorial or endowment-type gifts.

(6) Provide authoritative information about the federal income tax implications of every type of contribution.

ORGANIZATIONAL STRUCTURE MAY VARY

For institutions and denominations undertaking an effort along these lines, production of related printed material and enlistment of qualified staff people obviously is involved. Budget provision must be made accordingly. Simply by broadening areas of responsibility for some personnel and by creative utilization of existing specialized facilities, such as the church's already functioning accounting and investing services, it may be possible for a church body to institute a full scale program at relatively low cost.

On the local level, on the other hand, especially for those church bodies with "special gifts" agencies in their structures, budget costs will be trivial. The first thing for the local committee to do is to ascertain what helps and services are available within their denomination. Usually consultative assistance, printed material and visual aids are offered without charge or at nominal cost. The local committee is then free to devote its energies to putting these materials and services to as creative use as possible in the local situation.

The impression seems to be widely held that some kind of separate corporate structure, such as a "foundation," is needed before instituting a wills-emphasis program. In my view this is a mistaken impression. Another corporate entity is *not needed* for a congregation to receive bequests and special gifts. The congregation's structure as a religious organization is adequate for the reception of any kind of gift.

In my observation, where separate structures are envisioned, the creation of them becomes the preoccupation of a few, while the broad program of education never gets under way. The latter is the needful thing, not the former.

SERVICE APPROACH IS KEYNOTE

In the view of most persons experienced in this field, the place to start is with a wills-emphasis or wills-education program. This effort is the basic one. To a degree the other elements comprising the "program for action" are outgrowths or variations of it. I give major attention, therefore, to this phase of the work. Undertaken in a spirit of *education* and *service,* a wills program can be a rewarding experience for all who are reached by it.

THE NATURE OF WILLS PROMOTION

In tempo and in mood a wills program is apt to differ from other organized efforts within the congregation.

One church executive with long experience in this work has said, "A wills-emphasis program is best undertaken as a 'long-range, low-pressure type of educational program'—an effort which is never altogether finished and the results of which may never be fully known by the persons engaged in it."

A college official of an institution noted for the effectiveness of its bequests development program has stated, "A wills program should be characterized by (1) universality; (2) optimism, and (3) urgency."

By "universality" is meant having something to say to everyone, not just to a select few. It is as important for a young couple to have a will as for their elderly maiden aunt —usually more so insofar as consequences to loved ones when the deceased leaves no will.

By "optimism" is meant stressing the positive aspects of making a will. Referring to one's will as "our *first* will and testament" is a step in this direction; stressing the privilege and opportunity aspects of will-making are others.

By "urgency" is meant being mindful of the uncertainties of life. The best time to make a will is when a person is in good health.

WHAT DISTINGUISHES A CHRISTIAN'S WILL?

There can be many answers to such a question. This is one that appeals to me. I'm unable to acknowledge its authorship:

1. A Christian's will states or testifies that the maker believes in God. The testament may be as simple as "I believe in Almighty God," or it may be a more extended expression of the will-maker's faith. Some attorneys, as a matter of personal practice, begin wills with "In the name of God. Amen." By this simple act they acknowledge that the making of a will is something other than a routine business transaction.

2. A Christian's will makes fair, sensible and adequate provisions for the maker's loved ones in accordance with their needs and the size of the estate involved.

3. A Christian's will makes known the maker's wishes on matters such as the type of funeral desired; whether the maker desires to be interred or desires to be cremated; the kind of monument, if any, to be placed with the remains; the dear friends to whom he desires to leave an especially treasured keepsake, and the "good turn" known only to himself, but which he earnestly desires to repay.

4. A Christian's will remembers God by leaving a portion of the estate, no matter how small that portion may be, to further the work of God through a worthy church.

WHAT ORGANIZATION IS NEEDED
TO PROMOTE WILLS IN THE CONGREGATION?

Organization for a wills-emphasis program in a congregation usually consists of a wills-emphasis committee and a wills-advisory committee.

The wills-emphasis committee may be a subcommittee of

the congregation's stewardship committee. If the stewardship committee is already fully occupied, an entirely new committee should be authorized by the church council. The purpose of this committee is to plan and promote the whole wills effort.

A small number of dedicated and interested men and women of middle or advanced years makes the best committee. From two to five persons, depending on the size of the congregation, is recommended.

They need not have special knowledge or experience in the legal aspects of wills or estates. In actual practice it has been observed that professionals in these fields, notably attorneys, bankers and trust officers, seem to prefer not to be too actively involved in the "promotional aspects" of the wills-emphasis program. On the other hand, such persons are quite willing to assist in other ways, for example, on a wills-advisory committee, whose function is to make available the technical advice and religious counsel necessary for the proper writing of wills in which the church is remembered.

Membership of this committee usually consists of two kinds of persons: some thoroughly acquainted with the church's work, both at home and at large, and some with special knowledge or experience in the legal or technical aspects of wills and estates. Religious counsel is best given by the pastor, church officers and other members experienced in the wider work of the church. Technical advice can be given by attorneys, bankers, trust officers, surrogate or probate court officials, insurance agents and public accountants.

It should always be made clear to the congregation that the wills-advisory committee *does not write wills.* Within legal ethics it may recommend someone who can. Information given by the advisory committee should always be "general" rather than "specific." Persons with specific problems of law should always be directed to their own legal counsel.

THINGS THE WILLS COMMITTEE CAN DO

The wills-emphasis committee should seek to do some or all of the following:

A. *Distribute printed matter about wills:*
   1. As enclosures in regular mailings to the congregation.
   2. As enclosures in special mailings to the congregation.
   3. As enclosures with the Sunday bulletin.
   4. As display items on the tract rack.
   5. As take-home pieces for persons attending meetings where this subject is presented as a program topic.

B. *Encourage "wills emphasis" as a program topic at regular or special meetings of adult groups within the congregation. The following are possibilities:*
   1. The church council (a good place to start).
   2. The women's auxiliary.
   3. The men's auxiliary.
   4. Family-night gatherings.
   5. Golden-age groups.
   6. The annual meeting of the congregation.
   7. Meetings especially arranged for this purpose.

C. *Assist individuals who desire further information or counsel:*
   1. "Interest cards," distributed at meetings where this subject is discussed or selectively mailed to members of the congregation, facilitate this part of the program; on these cards individuals may request "technical assistance" or "ministerial guidance," or both.
   2. Depending upon the response, the wills-emphasis committee may arrange individual appointments with members of the advisory committee, or arrange group meetings of persons with similar concerns.

D. *Make provision for periodic follow-up:*
   1. At least twice a year include a wills leaflet or tract in a general mailing to the congregation.
   2. Periodically place new wills material on the display rack.

3. Plan to repeat a congregation-wide emphasis about every third year; the membership of the congregation keeps changing; individual circumstances change, too—persons not receptive at first may be much more so the next time around.

4. Keep in mind that writing a will is in some ways like writing a letter which is never quite finished—persons need to be reminded to review their wills periodically; changed circumstances may offer new opportunities to remember the church.

GIVING-WHILE-LIVING

The making of capital gifts to church or charity by living donors, with right of income retained to the donor for life and with usage of the contributed sum by the beneficiary-entity deferred until after the donor's passing, may seem to be a relatively recent development. One well-known organization, the American Bible Society, however, has been receiving contributions of this character for more than a century, while some other organizations and churches have been receiving contributions in this way for 75 years or more.

The plan in longest and most extensive use is known as "gift annuity agreement." More recent developments have been arrangements called variously: "regular life income contract" or "agreement"; "tax-free life income agreement" or "tax-free trust," and "charitable remainder trust."

A brief description of each is herein set forth by courtesy of Sydney Prerau, editor, *Contributor's Income Tax Deduction Guide*, 1961-62 edition:

Gift Annuity In exchange for a lump sum payment (usually in amounts of at least $100.00 or $500.00) the church or charity agrees to issue an annuity to the donor. He receives a fixed dollar amount annually for the rest of his life. The annual amount is based upon his age at the time of the issuance of the annuity. The donor gets a contribution deduction for a determined amount in the same year. His annuity receipts are in part free from income tax. Rates offered by most institutions are those recommended by a triennial Conference on Gift Annuities. For single life agreements present rates range from 3.0% at age 35 to 7.4% at age 80 and over.

Life Income Contract The donor turns over money or property to the church or charity which agrees to pay him for life a percentage return on that amount equal to the percentage earned by its endowment fund. The donor has a contribution deduction but not for the contract amount. It must be discounted by the time lapse before the charity gets it. The amount of the discount depends upon the donor's age. This is computed by use of Government tables. When appreciated property is given the donor avoids the capital gains tax, and the fair market value of the property at the time of the contract is used to determine the contribution deduction.

Taxfree Trust Donor transfers money or property to a trust to invest the funds in tax-exempt bonds. The income from the bonds is paid to the donor for his life and upon his death the funds become the absolute property of the charity. The donor pays no income tax on his receipts from the trust. He has a contribution deduction which is figured in the same way as the life income contract.

Charitable Remainder Trust Donor transfers money or property to a trustee to hold the property, invest the same, and pay the income of the trust to the donor himself, his wife, or children individually or consecutively. Upon the death of the last designated income beneficiary, the trust principal becomes the property of a charitable organization. The donor has a charitable deduction for the present value of the trust principal which eventually goes to the charity. The value is determined by Government tables. This trust can be set up by the donor during his life or in his will.

AN AUTHORITATIVE OBSERVER CITED

For the newcomer to this field, somewhat bewildered by the apparent complexity of the terminology, may I offer a word of encouragement. Having only recently been a neophyte myself, I can testify that, as is the case with any new subject matter, that which seems hopelessly complex at the outset gradually becomes a part of one's "stock in trade." Actually this diversity of giving plans is not unlike an array of tools for a skilled workman. For him each tool has its special function or purpose. Likewise, the development officer knows which life income plan best meets the need or fulfills the intention of his donors.

The problem of complexity is somewhat clarified by asserting at the outset that the gift annuity agreement seems to best suit the needs and desires of most donors to religious organizations. In contrast, life income agreements, both regular and tax-free, appear to have had wider acceptance among donors to colleges and universities. There are exceptions, of course, but in the main this seems to be the case.

Charles W. Baas, treasurer of the American Bible Society, shared his vast experience in this regard at the Conference on Modern Christian Philanthropy, in Cleveland, Ohio, February 1961. Let his own words tell the story:

Here is a little report on a private survey which I believe to be reasonably accurate in reflecting the life income activities of church boards. [A matter of terminology: When I subsequently mention life income agreements, I am referring to all those agreements which are not gift annuities.] This survey revealed that most life income agreements included two people in their fifties as beneficiaries. The gift annuity average was entirely different. Annuitant age averaged slightly under seventy and usually included only one life per agreement. I am quite certain that many purchases of life income agreements have been brought about through concern for retirement protection. There is a real and growing need for such protection. In the United States, year 1900, there were only three million people sixty-five years of age and older, while today there are almost fifteen million in that same age group. There are some government predictions which indicate that the number of people aged sixty-five and over will reach twenty-one million by 1975. In other words, the portion of our population aged sixty-five and over is increasing at just about double the rate of our total population. This is certainly enough to get our older people thinking in terms of income which they cannot outlive.

My survey reveals that the regular life income agreement had an average value per donor of approximately $5,000, while the tax-free life income agreement had a value of over $15,000. The average of all life income agreements approximates $8,000 per agreement. This is in great contrast with gift annuities which averaged about $2,000 per donor. In spite of the lower average figure, gift annuities apparently account for a larger total dollar value than any other type of life income agreement.

DOES ANNUITY GIVING
INTERFERE WITH OTHER GIVING?

In connection with the Tenth Conference on Gift Annuities, held in New York in 1959, it was my responsibility to compile a report as to generally prevailing practices among gift annuity issuing agencies. To that end a survey form was distributed and replies assimilated. In the process, while reviewing minutes of earlier conferences, I discovered that people have been seeking answers for many years about all aspects of giving. Back in 1931, for example, the question was being asked, even as it is now, "Do annuity gifts to a charitable organization interfere with gifts to it in other ways?"

Reply was made to that question at that time by Ernest F. Hall, secretary, department of annuities, Presbyterian board of foreign missions. What was said then seems to me to be equally true of annuity-giving today. For that reason I quote his reply in full:

It is difficult to answer this question because organizations which are receiving gifts on the annuity plan do not know in most cases the financial ability of the donors. In a few cases, doubtless outright gifts could be made with no annuity return.

In other cases it would be absolutely impossible. Many letters have been received stating that the writers cannot make outright gifts, but they can take advantage of the annuity plan. Some persons who have given on the annuity plan have also from time to time made outright gifts. The annuity plan offers to many people of moderate means, especially those who are deeply interested in the work of an organization, an opportunity to make a gift which they might not otherwise be able to make. Many women of very limited means have counted it as a great a privilege to give to an organization a definite amount of money on the annuity plan and thus feel that they are, up to the limit of their ability, aiding the work of the society. It is very doubtful that the same amount of money which is received on the annuity plan would be received from the same sources as outright gifts, if the plan were not available.

In connection with the report of current practices, to which I referred, it seemed to me that another quote from the 1931 Conference on Gift Annuities was as valid now as when it was first said. Credited also to Mr. Hall, it was this:

Annuity gifts, as a rule, are not made by the wealthy, but by people of limited means in addition to what they voluntarily and gladly contribute each year to the current work of the organization.

In summary, several life income plans are being offered by religious, educational and welfare institutions. Generally speaking, for persons desirous of benefiting religious causes, the gift annuity plan seems to have enjoyed wider acceptance than the other plans suggested. To meet the need or circumstance of every donor, however, it will be well to offer more than the one plan. Reasons for the popularity of the gift annuity agreement as a vehicle for giving to churches or church-related agencies seem to be these:

1. Attractive rate of return.
2. Lifetime guarantee.

3. Income largely tax-free.
4. Significant tax-saving benefits in year transfer is made.
5. Freedom from investment responsibility.
6. Easiness to arrange by mail.
7. Satisfaction of making a lifetime capital gift for the Lord's work.

LIFE INSURANCE GIVING ON INCREASE

For many persons life insurance policies represent the most valuable property they own. Oftimes it works out that the contingency against which protection had been purchased years before never transpires. For the thoughtful Christian, periodically reviewing his estate plan, this may afford another opportunity to do something for his church he might not otherwise have done; for example, designating the church as ultimate beneficiary of policies no longer needed for other purposes.

Authorities tell us that an ever increasing amount of insurance is now being written to "pay off" to the insured during his lifetime rather than to others at his passing. Again, for some, when that point is reached, other holdings or income adequately provide for their foreseeable needs. Proceeds from maturing policies might well become the basis of a gift annuity, for example. By so doing, the church is given a more certain prospect of a gift than is accorded it by writing a bequest into a will; at the same time, it gives the formerly insured person the spiritual satisfaction of making a gift to a cause in which he is interested, as well as the practical benefit of a flow of income which he cannot outlive.

For persons of other circumstances—like so many these days, with good income prospects but with little likelihood of accumulating reserve funds that might someday be given away, the purchase of a policy for the express purpose of providing an "insurance bequest" may enable persons of relatively modest means to have the joy of making a "big gift."

New methods of underwriting have been developed whereby policies designated for religious or charitable purposes may be issued without medical examination, for persons aged from 20 to 65, in face amount of $1,000 or $2,000. An alternative arrangement offers the maximum principal value that may be purchased at a given age by premium payments of $50 or $100. At age 40, for example, for a $50 annual premium a male church member can assure his church an insurance bequest amounting to $1,639.

Premium payments under policies of this character, where no rights to ownership are retained to the insured, qualify as charitable contributions on the Federal Income Tax return on the insured.

A program of this character, developed by New York insurance man Philip J. Goldberg, has resulted in millions of dollars designated for Hebrew philanthropies. Comparable service is now being offered Protestant churches by an organization known as the Institute for Philanthropic Planning, Inc. Its organizer and director, Walter Mortensen, is an active member of a Lutheran congregation in Brooklyn, New York.

MEMORIAL GIFTS

This appealing assertion appears in one church's promotional piece on memorial giving: *"The best way to honor the departed is to serve the living."* A time-honored way of memorializing loved ones when death comes is to make a money gift to some worthy cause or enterprise. Depending on the amount involved, such gifts typically are either for immediate use or they are to be the basis of an endowment-type fund with only the income therefrom to be expended.

Funds of this latter category are usually established on an individual basis for a specified minimum amount, either $100 or $500. Larger amounts, of course, are more dramatically significant. A fund of $2,500, for example, producing income at the rate of 4 percent, assures the benefited agency an annual gift of $100. For some this may be the means through which annual giving is capitalized.

An appeal of memorial funds is that they can be established by outright contributions, by bequest, through life insurance or by designation of the remainder value from a life income gift.

In this connection, the point must be raised as to whether it is altogether in the best interests of the local congregation to have an endowment fund. Stewardship leaders generally agree that where such funds are present in large amount, the stewardship practices of the congregation tend to deteriorate.

Where it is possible to give direction to potentially interested donors, encourage them to direct the proceeds of their fund either to the enrichment of the congregational program, in contrast with its mere maintenance, or, better yet, to one of the great causes of the church for which additional support will always be helpful.

Most denominational special gift agencies offer facilities for receiving and administering gifts of this character. Usually this service is offered without administrative cost, either to the donor or to the fund, assuring the greatest possible usefulness from whatever yield results.

Chapter 6

INVESTING TO BUILD

DOES your church need money immediately for an expansion program or remodeling of a building? Then give serious consideration to the sale of church bonds.

FOUR TYPES OF BONDS

There are four types of bonds which may be sold by a church: (1) debenture bonds that are unsecured obligations of the church—there is no pledge, assignment or mortgage of property; (2) registered bonds that, as the name implies, are the possession of the owner and must be registered in the records of the seller—these may have coupons attached which are payable to the bearer or the interest may be paid by check; (3) callable bonds that are subject to call for payment anytime by the church—this may be an interest-saving device for the church in that it may feel capable of paying the bonds off before maturity; (4) coupon bonds that are negotiable bonds and may be cashed by the possessor—coupons are attached that indicate the dates for payment of interest; both bonds and coupons are transferrable without notification to the church.

Before entering into the sale of bonds, church officials should make full and complete inquiry to make certain they are legal in their community, and, where permissible, to make certain all legal steps have been taken.

INSTANT MONEY

As indicated above, when a church enters a bond-sale program, needed money is available at once. In the same time it takes to promote a building fund canvass to raise $150,000, to be paid over a 3-year period, a church can put on a bond sale program and raise the same amount immediately.

This sounds challenging and easy. Enthusiasm may be aroused by the possibility of raising the needed money at once, by stepping up the timetable of a building program at least three years, and by the ideas of extra income through investing the money which will not be needed until a later date. Such enthusiasm may make a church want to get going immediately. Before starting, however, give serious consideration to these observations.

Give deep and careful study to the amount of money to be raised through the sale of bonds. First thoughts may cause church officials to endorse a too ambitious program. There is a feeling that the sale of bonds will be easy, that the interest rate will lure many purchasers. Avariciousness causes stretching beyond financial possibility of the congregation.

There are two important words: *"Don't overreach!"* The best prospects are members of the church that is selling the bonds. A few nonmembers may be induced to invest, but the bond-sale program cannot be based on the hope of selling a large number of bonds to those not affiliated with the church. I repeat, members of the church are the best and most likely prospects. Therefore, an exhaustive survey of the financial potential of the members of the church should be made. Members in the high-income level are not the best prospects, unless the church pays 6- or 7-percent yield. If the interest must go that high, then it would be better not to have the bond issue. On the other hand, if the bonds do not return a good yield, then those in the high-income bracket may not be interested because they can make more profitable investments.

Members in the middle-income group are better prospects. It is true these people do not usually have much extra money. Many are paying for a house, a car, a boat or furniture. Others are sending their children to college. In spite of these obligations, many are able to put some money aside. If the church offers 5 or 5½ percent on the bonds, some of this money will be diverted to the church.

Families of low income are poor prospects, because most of these families spend every cent they get. Savings is an unknown quantity for most of them. Consequently, it is difficult to sell bonds to these people, devoted and sincere as they may be. It is not that they will not, but they cannot. Therefore, a thorough investigation should be made of the potential of the congregation before selling bonds. Just how this information is attained is a matter for the local congregation.

In a small or medium-size church this information is usually known. The members of the church are well enough acquainted with each other that officials can quickly decide what the size of the bond issue should be. In larger churches, especially in metropolitan areas, such information is more difficult to attain. Nevertheless, time spent in determining the potential of the congregation is both time and money earned. It can prevent embarrassment and failure at a later date.

DANGERS AND BENEFITS

Without this investigation the officials may decide to go far beyond the potential of the congregation. This is over-reaching and several things may happen. First, the whole venture may fall on its face in complete failure. This could cause such a feeling of frustration among the church members that the progress of the church could be set back for years. Second, the congregation may be so hounded to purchase bonds that they wish they had never heard of them. This causes a negative attitude to the bond selling idea, not only in the church involved, but in other congregations where a bond program could be effective but will not be tried. Third, it may be embarrassing to officials of the church because they find it necessary to go to outsiders to purchase the excess bonds.

I am aware of one church that had the tragic experience of having to resort to outside help. The sale of bonds was endorsed by the church without determining how much could be absorbed by the congregation. A goal of $250,000 was set. The bonds were put out for sale. After purchasing about $175,000 of the bonds, the membership ran out of funds. The officials of the church kept prodding, they kept annoying the members, and tried all means to sell the remainder. Eventually they turned to other sources. They tried the public at large, through newspaper advertisements; they went to stock brokers trying to interest them in purchasing some of the bonds; they went to local banks asking them to take some. For months there was frustration and desperation in the church.

After much hard work and many hours of running, all the bonds were sold. Then came another time of hardship. The congregation had to pay back to the lenders. They found this was absorbing a greater percentage of their income than it should. Consequently, other phases of the church's work were suffering. Members were becoming discouraged and leaving the church. New residents in the community were uniting with other churches not so heavily burdened with debt. This church has suffered loss of growth and effectiveness that will take years to overcome, because sufficient time was not taken to determine the potential of the congregation.

When a congregation sells bonds, it borrows money from

itself for itself. Instead of borrowing from a lending institution, the officials of the church turn to their own fellow members and say, "We would like to borrow the money from you."

There are several benefits in this plan. One, the rate of interest paid on the bonds may be, and usually is, lower than the rate of interest paid to a lending institution. This difference in rate of interest may amount to thousands of dollars saved by the church over the course of years.

Another benefit is that the money received from the bond sales may in turn be used as a source of income for the church. Since the money is available at once, but may not be used immediately, it may be invested in a savings institution at a reasonable interest rate. This income will help the church pay some of its own obligations on the bonds.

One church, for instance, sold a $150,000 issue of bonds. The money came in much more rapidly than it was needed. Rather than have it in a checking account, where only the bank would benefit from it, the officials of the church decided to transfer the money to savings and loan associations where they would receive one percent per quarter on the money. The money was invested in these associations up to the insured limit. Thus, the church was realizing some return on its own investment.

One other benefit is that the church can proceed at once with the project for which the money is intended. There is no necessity to wait several years as in the case of a 3-year building fund drive. With the sale of bonds the money is at hand, and plans may go forward at once.

INSTANT DEBT

A word of warning is in order. As soon as a congregation sells bonds it is *in debt!* For instance, if a congregation sells $100,000 in bonds within six weeks, then within that six weeks the church has gone in debt to the amount of $100,000, plus interest. Or to say it another way, a debt-free church at the beginning of May could conceivably be "way down under" by the end of June. This result of bond sales should be uppermost in the minds of church officials. It is a quick way of raising money; it is a quick way of going into debt.

OBJECTIONS TO BONDS

Some denominational stewardship directors object to the sale of bonds by churches. They maintain that it mitigates against stewardship and defeats the purpose of stewardship teaching. I recall an incident during one of the sessions at the Center for Church Business Management, The American University, Washington, D.C. A stewardship secretary of a large denomination sat in the session during which bond sales were being discussed. He had not noticed that this was the topic for the hour or, according to his own words, he would not have been present. All through the opening statement he sat impatiently waiting to get into the discussion. When he had the opportunity, he stated in no uncertain terms his staunch opposition to bond sales because he felt it was against everything for which good stewardship stands.

My feeling is that we are not in the realm of stewardship, as usually interpreted, when we are in a bond selling program. This is business and should be handled in a business-like manner. For instance, a church needs $100,000. Authority has been given to the officials to borrow said amount. Two means for getting these funds are available: Go to a commercial lending institution to borrow the money, or go to the congregation with bonds—borrow money from the membership.

The decision is made to tap this latter source. I do not see where stewardship enters into this. If the officials of the church had gone to a lending institution to get the money, it is a loan, repayable so much per month over a stated number of years at a given amount of interest. The officers of the institution may be members of the church, many of the members of the church may have some of their money invested in the institution, but we do not talk to these commercial lenders about stewardship. It is a loan, legal, businesslike and repayable.

In turn, if the church officers go to the congregation to sell bonds to raise the necessary funds, this, too, is a loan, repayable over a given number of years. In the sense that all of life is stewardship, this is stewardship, also. Strictly speaking, bond sales are not contrary to stewardship.

In my opinion, the accusation that bond sales interfere with stewardship is another way of saying that if we sell bonds the members will not give. If this is true, then those responsible for the sale of the bonds have not properly instructed the congregation. In purchasing a bond nothing is given to the church. The money is invested in the church and the investment will bring a suitable return. Eventually the money will be returned as the bonds mature. Giving to the church continues. In fact, after the sale of bonds, increased giving is necessary. There is no interference with stewardship.

BONDS VERSUS PLEDGES

There is a related question which is frequently raised: Should a bond-sales program take the place of an every-member canvass for a building fund or capital improvements? My answer is that rather than being "in place of," one may supplement the other. One church made good use of both plans: Expansion would be essential within five years. To be financially prepared, a building-fund canvass was conducted with pledges to be paid over three years. After pledges had been paid for two years a substantial amount of money was available but not enough to begin building. It was decided to have a sale of bonds so more money would be available at once. This was done with great success. The building was actually under way two and one-half years ahead of schedule.

In the meantime, the third-year pledges continued to be paid to the building fund. At the end of the three years, with the building completed, the building debt became a part of the church budget. The amount of the pledges for expansion was added to pledges for current expenses. There was one pledge for one budget. Therefore, the building-fund canvass three years earlier became a supplement to the bond-sales program, for the increased giving made possible the repayment of the debt caused by sale of the bonds and what had been borrowed from a lending institution.

BOND SELLING ETHICS

Another important matter needs to be brought to attention here. A church should never sell bonds with the idea that those who purchase them, especially members of the church, will give the interest coupons to the church or donate the bonds to the church when they mature. In fact, I have had church leaders suggest that this is one of the virtues of the bond program. To me, this is exploiting the membership. First, we say loan the money to your church; then, we ask how can you want to have your money returned when you know how much we need it. Bond sales are strictly a business proposition, entered into in good faith. When the debt is due, pay it! Do not expect a kickback!

This is not meant to discourage the donation of bonds or interest coupons to the church. Some members will find it useful to do so for income tax purposes. Others may use their coupons and bonds to pay their pledges to the church. But this is voluntary and unexpected.

However, if the church officials make known that this is expected of bond purchasers, then I believe a serious ethical breach has been committed. It puts members in the embarrassing position of giving what they cannot afford. To some it may mean sacrificing money saved for their children's education. To some it may jeopardize their retirement, and to all it could prove an awkward situation.

Sell the bonds for investment purposes. Pay the interest as it comes due. Pay the bonds off as they mature. Keep the whole transaction on good business principles.

CONDUCTING A BOND SELLING PROGRAM

Let us draw the loose ends together by going into detail about the promotion of a bond-sales program, the maturity schedules, the bonds themselves, the sinking fund, security of bonds and other pertinent information.

The easiest way to dispose of this is to say to those thinking of a bond-sales program, "Contact one of the several professional companies who do this sort of work. It will save you much trouble and short-cut what could otherwise be a circuitous route."

I realize this is not a satisfactory answer. I am aware, also, that many who are interested may not contact one of these firms until some preliminary questions are answered. Therefore, I shall give some details, but within the scope of this chapter it is impossible to go into minute particulars. Furthermore, each situation has its own peculiarities.

Briefly let us review three important steps: be certain the members of the church will support such a program; determine a safe amount to be raised—do not overreach; make certain that proper authority has been given by the church to the officials responsible for the program. Once these matters have been taken care of, then you may proceed.

In some states it is necessary to petition the local court with a detailed resolution before bonds can be offered for sale. Among other things, this resolution goes into detail relative to the bonds, their maturity, indebtedness on the church, the ability of the congregation to carry the debt and related information. One purpose of the resolution is to give protection to bond purchasers. After being passed by the court, it is then recorded and is open to all who may wish to read it. If your state requires this action, do not take any further steps until it has been done.

As for the bonds themselves, they should be attractively printed, beautifully embossed, on good paper so they give the appearance of being a valuable possession, which they are. On the face of the bond is the name of the church issuing it, the amount of the bond, the interest rate, the total number of bonds in the issue, the total amount of money to be raised, the prepayment privilege, a statement giving protection to the holder of the bond, the signatures of officers of the church. Attached to each bond are the required number of coupons for the life of the bond.

It is very important that the purchaser of the bond be informed that it is negotiable—meaning that if lost or stolen the bearer may redeem it. This may avoid carelessness and prevent a great deal of work by the issuing institution in case the bond must be replaced.

The bonds may be issued in any denomination desired by the church. The most common are $50, $100, $250, $500 and $1,000. The circumstances of the church families will help determine the number of bonds in each denomination to be issued. That is, in some congregations there may be calls for many $100 bonds but few $1,000 bonds. In other situations there may be many calls for $500 and $1,000 bonds, but none for $50 bonds.

The interest rate should be high enough to make it worthwhile for the members to make the investment. However, it should not be so high that it would be above what would be paid by a commercial lending institution.

The maturity dates may range from one and one-half years to fourteen years. Once more, this will be determined by the local church but these periods have been found acceptable. The maturity dates are so arranged that no great number of bonds come due at any one time, thus relieving any undue strain on the church treasury.

To retire the bonds the church creates a sinking fund in a local bank by special arrangement with the bank. Some banks will charge for this service and rightly so because it does require extra work for bank personnel. Other banks will give the service free as a public relations project.

Each week, the church treasurer will deposit in this sinking fund an amount sufficient to pay the bonds and the interest as they come due. The amount to be deposited is determined by the following formula: For the first six months after the sale of the bonds, $1 a week is deposited for each $1,000 of bonds in the issue; beginning with the seventh month and continuing until full maturity of the bonds, $2 a week are deposited for each $1,000 of the issue. For instance, if the amount of the issue is $100,000, then for the first six months $100 a week is deposited. Beginning with the seventh month, $200 a week is deposited. This amount being deposited each week will be sufficient to pay all interest and the bonds as they mature. NOTE: The deposit is made on the basis of the amount of the issue, not on the amount sold.

This money must be the first paid out every week. A church wishing to be honest with its bondholders cannot procrastinate by waiting until the next week and making a double deposit. Bonds have first claim on all income and must be the first expenditure each week. If some indebtedness must wait, it should not be the sinking fund at the bank.

In many instances the security for the bonds is the income of the church, not the church property. One church which had so secured its bonds by such an arrangement found itself in a financial strain. Because of the treasurer's concern over paying other bills he forgot to make regular deposits into the sinking fund. By the time the error had been discovered the church was in debt to the bank several thousand dollars. Fortunately, the bank officials were considerate enough to advance the money, otherwise the whole bond program might have been put in jeopardy.

Once arrangements have been made with the bank and the sinking fund has been established, the bank becomes the paying agent. This takes a tremendous responsibility from the church. Once the bonds have been sold, the church is no longer concerned about them except to see that the deposits are made regularly. The bank will cash the coupons and the bonds. The procedure is similar to that of a checking account. The depositor keeps enough money in the bank to pay all the checks he draws against his account. The bank honors the checks and pays the money out. The same principle is involved here. By making regular deposits, the church keeps enough money in the sinking fund to pay bonds and interest as they come due, and, as with a checking account, the bank makes a regular accounting to the church.

IN CASE A MORTGAGE ALREADY EXISTS

A further statement needs to be made here pertaining to the collateral for the bonds. In some instances the property may be mortgaged as security. In this way the bondholders have a first mortgage on the property. Frequently, however, a lending institution holds a first mortgage on the buildings. What happens if the church desires to have a sale of bonds in spite of the mortgage? In such instance the church officials confer with the lending institution to learn whether or not they object to the bond sale. Usually there is no objection because they have first claim against the property and as long as the sale of bonds does not mitigate against their loan, they will give consent.

This raises a further problem. If there is a first mortgage against the property, does this mean that bondholders have a second mortgage? If so, then this becomes a poor risk and few people are willing to buy second trust notes unless the interest rate is high enough to warrant the added risk. There-fore, the bonds are not second mortgages, but are first claims on all income. It is important, therefore, as stated earlier, that the first money taken out of the church income each week is that which is deposited in the sinking fund. This money is mortgage money and belongs to the bondholders.

SALES CAMPAIGN PROCEDURE

Let us turn to the actual sales campaign itself. The sales organization is set up in the same manner as the organization for an every-member canvass. Training and orientation meet-ings are a must for those participating in the campaign. Dur-ing these meetings complete information and instruction should be given so that those calling on prospective pur-chasers, and this means every family in the church, will be able to answer questions and make the sale. Every salesman should make his own purchase before trying to sell others. We cannot sell that in which we do not believe.

Every worker should be provided with an information booklet in which would be the following, along with other information:

1. What the worker should know about the sales program.
2. What he should know about the bonds.
3. How to prepare for the visit, through study and reading and preparation of his mind and spirit.
4. How to make the visit, what to say, how to help prospect determine size of bond to purchase.
5. How to bring sale to successful conclusion.
6. How to make report of sale.

In addition, the worker should carry with him a letter of introduction signed by the minister and general chairman. The letter should be on church stationery, properly dated, reading as follows:

To Whom it May Concern:

This will introduce (name of worker), authorized representative of the Ever-Growing Methodist Church Bond Sales Program. This volunteer worker will outline our bond program and demonstrate how these bonds will not only build a new educational unit, but can be the basis of a sound savings and investment program for your future.

Sincerely,

Minister

Chairman, Bond Sales Organization

He should carry a bond reservation order form for each prospect on whom he calls. This form has the following information:

Total purchase $——————
Indicate the number of bonds of each denomination purchaser desires: no preference ——; $1000 ——; $500 ——; $250 ——; $100 ——; $50 ——.
List maturity dates in order of preference: 1. —— 2. ——
    3. —— 4. ——
Method of payment: —— in full; will pay in full on ——————
    196—; C.O.D. on —————— 19—; other —————— (Please
    give additional information and instructions on reverse side.)
Name of purchaser ——————————————
Address of purchaser ——————————————
Phone number of purchaser ——————————————
Date of purchase ——————————————
Order taken by ——————————————
Purchaser's signature ——————————————

With this form the salesman should have a receipt which may be left with the purchaser for any amount that has been collected.

The salesman should also have a bank credit application

with a self-addressed, stamped envelope. There will be some families in the church who will want to purchase some of the bonds, not only as an investment, but to help their church reach its goal. However, they may not have the cash immediately available. Through previous arrangement with the bank by the church officials, the prospective purchaser may borrow any part of the amount necessary to purchase a bond or bonds. The bank may charge anywhere from 4 to 6 percent on the loan and may extend the payments over as long as 36 months. Actually, the interest charge will be negligible to the bondholder because he will be receiving at least 5 percent from the church for the money he borrowed from the bank to purchase the bond. In fact, one bank showed that borrowing to purchase bonds was profitable. For instance, if $90 were borrowed to purchase a $100-bond, these are the results: total note $94.68, monthly payments (twelve months) $7.89, interest and insurance $4.68, bond dividends $5.00, profit $.32. Or if the bond purchaser borrowed $900 in order to purchase a $1,000-bond, the results are: total note $1,042.92, monthly payments (36 months) $28.97, interest and insurance $142.92, bond dividends, $150.00, profit $7.08.

After the loan to the bank is paid off, the bondholder will profit from the transaction because he will continue to receive the interest on the bond from the church.

This loan service is established as a service to the prospective purchaser. If he prefers, he may do business with his own bank.

Another important tool for each worker is an availability list. This list shows the total number of bonds available in each denomination, the number reserved, the number sold, the number still procurable, the denomination of the bond, the number of years to maturity and the maturity date. This list must be kept up to date so the worker will know at all times what bonds are available, thus avoiding the embarrassing situation of the same bond being promised or sold to two or more purchasers. This necessitates the prompt reporting of sales to and constant contact with the central office.

In the central office at the church, the secretary keeps an issue control sheet. On this sheet the bonds are listed serially beginning with the highest denomination in column one, and in subsequent columns the following information: years of maturity, date of maturity, name of person reserving the bond, amount of money received when order is given, the salesman, date of reservation. When the sale has been completed, this information: the purchaser, the total amount paid for the bond, the date the sale was made.

A brochure for general distribution should be printed. This may be as large or as small as a church wishes to make it. There may be many pictures or few. However, it should have these components: a statement of purpose, a statement of the need requiring the money, a statement of membership growth, a financial statement showing cost of the proposed program and sources of financing, with a strong closing statement which will make the prospect become a purchaser and proud possessor of a bond.

It goes without saying that a record of the purchasers will be kept in the church files. Since the bonds are negotiable and may be sold by the owner at his discretion, it is not always possible to keep up to date with such sales. However, the initial sales should be recorded and kept in permanent form. Subsequent changes may be made if the information is available. This permanent record should list the bonds by serial number, denomination, maturity date, name and address of the purchaser, date of purchase, and should have a place for remarks.

NOTHING NEW

The use of bonds to raise finances for church programs is not new. For more than a quarter of a century, churches have been using the plan or ideas similar to it, such as issuing notes to members for money borrowed. It has been successful in thousands of churches, both large and small. Many millions of dollars have been raised. The amazing fact in all of this is there have been very few defaults in payments and what defaults there have been are negligible.

CONSIDER THESE

For any church planning to go into a bond selling project, consider that it is a quick way to raise money; it is a quick way to go into debt; be certain you have the resources to repay your obligations. After this consideration and after you have decided to do it, move ahead with speed and may God bless you with success.

Chapter 7

KNOWING
YOUR DESTINATION

TODAY many problems confront our churches. Some of these are problems over which they have little or no control and others are of their own making. There are spiraling costs, deflated dollars and fixed giving on the one hand; apathy, complacency and procrastination on the other.

Membership in the local church has all too often become a "status symbol." "Token giving" has become the standard.

Add to these problems the threat of atheistic countries which are dedicated in large part to the destruction of our way of living and worshiping and you have a truly ominous picture.

To successfully overcome these problems, much realistic revaluation must take place. First, churches must abandon their historic role as a citadel, a haven of protection and become instead a launching platform for a dynamic militant force for the spreading of the Kingdom of God.

Churches are not ordained to operate budgets only, but to provide a program of (1) evangelism, (2) education, (3) service and (4) missions. These are the primary tasks. Budgets must be thought of in terms of what they can do to glorify God and bless the giver. Budget planning must be done with the thought in mind of "What would we do if we had all the money we wanted? How much faster could we win the world to Christ if we had better tools, more missions, etc?" rather than "How little can we get along on this year?"

Money must be understood for what it really is—not a "nasty word" but one of the most powerful tools available for the work of the church.

Given unlimited funds, Christianity could possibly win the world within our lifetime. These funds are available, not from foundations or government grants, but within the church itself. An aggressive, strong financial program in a local church will challenge and attract strong leadership. The impact of the powerful stewardship appeal will be felt in years to come in the increased level of spiritual participation and increased standard of giving.

The financing of a church budget is not an easy job. This is graphically illustrated by the modest budgets and low level of giving in many churches. In this country we have the highest standard of living in the world. Each Sunday, church parking lots are filled with expensive cars and in many cases the cost of the wardrobe worn by each family each Sunday far exceeds the amount of money given to the church during a year. In these same churches the finance committees are hard-pressed to finance even a modest budget.

Today raising church funds is a task of major proportions and many times churches are unable to find men in their own membership either qualified or with enough time to direct and conduct an every-member visitation or building-fund canvass.

To meet this problem, many churches are using the services of fund-raising organizations specializing in the field of church finance. The ability of these organizations is bringing into sharper focus the concept of Christian stewardship, and the encouragement of greater congregational participation in a stewardship program has been the turning point in the spiritual life of many churches.

These fund-raising organizations fundamentally attempt to reach, inform and inspire each member to the spiritual impact of stewardship. It is important to emphasize the need of each Christian to be a sacrificial giver and to bring home to each family that stewardship is the dynamo which powers all church activity. Many believe the spiritual level of a church can be measured in direct ratio to the degree to which stewardship is practiced in that church.

The canvass director is himself a dedicated Christian, highly trained in the various phases of fund-raising procedures and committed to a policy of stewardship within the church. His wide experience enables him to bring to the canvass the most important "do's" and "don't's." He devotes all of his time week after week to the job at hand. There is no division between outside interests and the canvass. His interest is the canvass at all times.

Because the director is not a member of the congregation, he is able to initiate, implement and carry to its conclusion a strong stewardship program without fear of criticism.

When leaders of a church organize their own canvass they are confronted with procedures that leave them open to criticism. Many times these criticisms are from people who give very little and have no real feeling of responsibility toward the church. Faced with these criticisms the leaders have a tendency to modify and water down their plans until there is little strength left in the program.

Furthermore, church leaders who attempt their own canvasses are subject to differences of opinion among themselves and must tactfully settle these differences by adding unproductive detours or accepting disastrous shortcuts. With outside help, the responsibility for the methods to be used rests on the director so that the program moves forward on schedule to its ultimate success.

Good canvass direction is not a substitute for anything the church would do on its own. It is rather a plus factor which produces a higher standard of giving, more pledging families, more effective use of leaders, a stronger organization and finally more satisfaction and enjoyment for those who participate.

When professional help is sought in all other walks of life, why not use professional help in an event as important as raising increased funds for the Kingdom of God?

PROPER APPROACH TO CANVASS

The most important factor in the success of an every-member canvass is the attitude with which it is approached. One attitude is, "Here we go again, begging for money" or "Let's hurry and finish this so we can get back to Christian work." The entire matter is treated as if it were a necessary but unpleasant "booster shot" to keep the church in business a little longer. Another attitude is, "We're not really doing so badly. After taking everything into consideration we're doing pretty well." With this philosophy permeating the church, you find a weak, ineffective canvass.

There should be a positive attitude in an every-member canvass—when Christians make their commitment to Christ through their pledges to further His kingdom. This will bring to each a richer and deeper understanding of stewardship.

There is no easy way to conduct an every-member canvass. It is a difficult task, but when properly conducted it is one of the most rewarding Christian experiences a church can have.

EVERY-MEMBER CANVASS

In general, there are three distinctive phases in an every-member canvass. Some of these will tend to overlap, but each must be complete in itself and each is essential to the success of the canvass. There is no little or unimportant job in any canvass. Like bricks in a foundation, each phase must be securely in place before the next is put in position.

The initial phase of the canvass takes place some weeks prior to the actual start of the canvass itself. During this period, the pastor, church staff and key leaders will meet to determine church potential, establish canvass goals, choose canvass leadership, prepare a canvass calendar and, in general, set the background for the intensive canvass period.

The second phase, the intensive canvass period, will take anywhere from three to ten or more weeks, depending upon the size of the church. Approximately 70 percent of this time is used in preparation for the actual call in the home. During this period, promotional, inspirational and informational materials are prepared. Workers are enlisted and trained. This phase begins with the first meeting of the canvass director and organizational leaders and ends with the last report meeting.

The third phase is the post-canvass period. This phase begins after the last report meeting and continues until the next intensive visitation, whether one year or five years later. Early in this phase a committee is established to send acknowledgment letters to all who pledged, giving the result of the canvass and confirming each commitment. During this phase another committee will be responsible for securing pledges from new members, from families not seen during the canvass period, from families asking to be seen later and from families who declined to pledge during the initial pledging period. This committee gives year-round impetus to the stewardship program. It may be a part of the church finance committee.

THE CANVASS ORGANIZATION

The canvass organization is the backbone of any successful visitation endeavor. Much care and thought must be used in choosing the members of this group. These workers will represent the church and its ideals in their contacts with church families. They must be enthusiastic, committed to and practicing stewardship, and filled with a sense of urgency regarding the church program. In addition they must be able to communicate these sentiments with great impact to each family visited. In this way all church members will be exposed to the principles of Christian stewardship.

In an every-member visitation, it is essential that workers are enlisted who are in full sympathy with the church program. Cold or lukewarm members can be more harmful than any other cause to the canvass. Each canvass member is a "teacher," consequently anyone not sufficiently convinced of the worth of the church program will be a very poor tool in the hands of God to bring others to a complete commitment. It is to be admitted that some men who had been skeptical at first have been brought into canvass organizations, and after hearing the details, have become enthusiastic supporters. On the whole, there is risk involved with these members.

Bluntness is needed frequently to make the workers come to a decision about their attitude. One general chairman announced to the training session of canvassers that if there were any who were not willing to make a sacrificial pledge, or any who were not in sympathy with the goal, they should leave because they would not contribute to the success of the canvass.

The purpose of this organization is twofold: first, to be properly trained to tell the story of the church program with assurance and clarity; second, to visit in the homes of each member of the church, to inform them of the goal and purpose of the canvass and to inspire them to make a sacrificial pledge to the program.

Following is a typical organizational chart of an every-member canvass. This may be modified, depending upon the type of canvass and size of church.

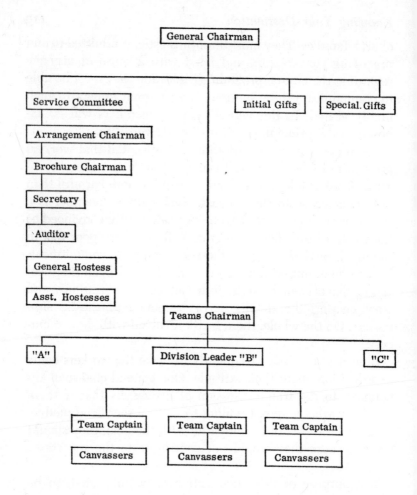

DUTIES OF THE CANVASS ORGANIZATION

The general chairman is the lay leader of the canvass organization. He is chosen for his devotion, his adherence to the principles of stewardship, his leadership qualities and his influence among the leaders of the church. He will preside at all committee meetings and assist in the selection of other key officers. At all times he will stand ready to bolster any weakness in the structure of the organization.

The initial gifts chairman has the responsibility of securing the pledges of the entire canvass organization prior to the start of the actual canvassing. He will get the pledges of the general chairman, the minister, the special gifts chairman and the teams chairman. He will follow through to make sure these men get the pledges of those who work with them. No one who has not himself made his sacrificial pledge should make any canvass calls.

In the case of a building-fund canvass, especially in a larger church, a *special gifts chairman* should be chosen. The chairman of this committee should himself be one of the most generous givers. His committee will be charged with the responsibility of contacting those members who are in a high-income bracket for the purpose of obtaining large, pace-setting pledges. The minimum pledge figure for this group can be left up to the discretion of the canvass committee. Too much stress cannot be put on the importance of this chairman and his committee members being among the larger and more generous givers. Only those who think big financially can challenge others to think big financially. Furthermore, it is disastrous to send a man who works in the office to go see the president of the firm. At this point there is class distinction. Men of a particular financial level should be visited by men of the same level.

The teams chairman is the supervisor of the general soliciting organization composed of the division leaders, the team captains and the canvassers. All prospects other than initial gifts and special gifts are handled by this group. The teams chairman, in consultation with minister and other leaders, will select qualified persons for the division leaders. He will coordinate the work of the division leaders and aid them in the selection of team captains. The teams chairman is the key to the success of the general organization. His leadership and devotion are vital.

The teams chairman is responsible for receiving the

pledges of his division leaders. However, he does not solicit them until he has submitted his own pledge. Let it be noted, also, that all of these pledges should be gotten from the workers in their homes. This makes the pledge a family pledge rather than that of only one member of the family.

The division leaders, in conjunction with the teams chairman, have the responsibility of selecting the team captains for the canvass. The size of the organization and the number of team captains will be determined by the size of the church. The division leaders will be responsible for the attendance at each training session and at the report meetings. The division leaders will solicit the pledges of their team captains after they have given their own pledges to the teams chairman.

The team captains will work directly with the canvassers. They must have a clear understanding of the aims of the canvass and the need of the giver to give for his own spiritual growth. It is their responsibility to impart this understanding to their team members.

The team captains, in consultation with the division leaders and teams chairman, select the names of qualified men they would like to have as members of their teams. They will call them personally and discuss with each individual his place in the canvass.

The team captains coordinate the work of the members of their teams, assist in their training, and knit them into a smooth-functioning organization. They confirm their attendance prior to each canvass meeting and are responsible for attendance at all training meetings. They will, upon request, assist any of their team members in their calls. The team captains are responsible for getting the pledges of each of their team members. No worker should be allowed to go into the homes of the membership at large without having first submitted his pledge to the canvass goal.

The canvassers are chosen upon the basis of their potential giving ability and their dedication to the principles of stewardship. These canvassers are mobilized into teams and are trained for their respective responsibilities. In general, about one canvasser for every five families is desirable.

The publicity chairman and his committee have the responsibility of accomplishing the following objectives: establishment of a "theme" for the canvass, preparation and distribution of a brochure outlining the canvass and giving the objectives in full.

The brochure should be organized to follow a logical sequence from the early history of the church through future plans. When properly organized it will give the complete picture of church planning and serve as a guide for the canvasser when he calls in the home. The outer cover should have some attractive design or a picture of the church, with the name and address of the church. The inside cover may be blank or have a verse of scripture or poetry on it.

Next should be a letter from the minister, along with his picture.

Then there should be a brief history of the church, followed by a statement of the need. The latter may take several pages; however, an important part of this section is to include many pictures. There should be little script. One picture will tell the equivalent of hundreds of words. Furthermore, if there is too much print, it will not be read.

Next make a statement of the plan to meet the need. Here there may be a floor plan. Floor plans are not always understood, so their inclusion is not important. This should be followed with several pages on the financial status of the church, the financial goal of the present canvass and, most important, some figures on the responsibility of the individual member. One page may be given over to a facsimile of the pledge card to be used.

Close out with an inspirational poem or appropriate scripture quotation. The back cover may be left blank. These brochures may be as simple or as ornate as the church finances will allow. Under all circumstances, however, there should be a brochure.

The publicity committee will be responsible for keeping the church membership informed about the progress of the canvass, for developing interest in the unqualified success of the canvass and for helping the membership to answer the most important of all canvass questions, "How much should I give?" In general, it should create an atmosphere in which the canvasser will be welcomed at every call.

The arrangements chairman and committee are responsible for the location and serving of the Loyalty Dinner which is the highlight of the canvass. The success of the Loyalty Dinner can determine to what degree the canvass will succeed.

In addition, this committee is responsible for the care and entertainment of premembership children the night of the Loyalty Dinner and for the provision of refreshments at the report meetings.

In arranging the Loyalty Dinner, brevity is the key. There will be six or seven speakers limited from five to ten minutes each, depending on their topic. If possible they should meet several days before the dinner to coordinate their talks, to avoid overlapping and to check on the timing. The following is a suggested program:

Time	Subject	Leader
7:00	Call to Order	Master of ceremonies.
7:01	Invocation	Pastor.
7:02	Dinner	Not by ladies of the church; catered or served in some other church.
8:00	Introductions	Master of ceremonies.
8:05	Our Church—History	An older member.

8:15	Our Needs	One acquainted with the needs calling for the canvass.
8:25	Our Plan	General chairman or canvass chairman.
8:35	Our Responsibility	A generous supporter of the church, perhaps a tither.
8:45	How to Make a Pledge	Member of finance committee or teams chairman.
8:55	Inspirational Address and Benediction	Pastor.
9:00	Adjournment	

In asking members of the congregation to participate in the program, the following suggestions may be given to them to help in developing their talks.

For the speaker on "History of the Church," let him briefly give the history, telling some of the struggles it has had, mentioning some of the people connected with its development, such as former ministers and outstanding members now gone. Give present membership figures. He may say something about the mission of this particular church to the community. He must stay away from any subjects that will be discussed by others in the program.

The speaker on "Our Needs" will point up the things that have brought about the canvass. His talk, therefore, will be developed according to the need. If it is an educational unit being built, he will discuss the Sunday school, kindergarten, scouts, adult and youth needs. If it is a nave or sanctuary, he will talk about the worship services, the choirs and related needs. He will lift up the financial requirements to meet the physical needs.

The speaker on "Our Plan" will keep in mind that the

former speaker has been stressing the needs. He will tell what the plan is to meet these needs: First, every member-family and as many of the "users" as possible will be visited for pledges. Second, at no time will there be public solicitation of funds; all pledges will be received in the homes. Third, the canvasser will be a fellow member of the church and frequently a neighbor. Fourth, only subscriptions are being asked for, not cash gifts. Fifth, he will stress the need for sacrificial giving, not for the finances alone but for what it means to the giver.

The speaker on "Our Responsibility" will point out that it is the responsibility of the members and friends of the church to meet the needs described by the preceding speaker. Let him show that there are some phases of the Christian work that will not be accomplished if we do not assume our responsibilities. The canvass is organized to be a united and concentrated effort on the part of all member-families, thus avoiding the necessity of a few bearing the load.

The speaker on "How to Make a Pledge" will have a chart of weekly giving and the pledge card at hand. He will be definitely concerned with the questions, "How much should I give?" and "What is a sacrificial gift to me?" He should refer to the chart of weekly giving so members may see their potential beginning at the high and proceeding to the low. He should talk about the pledge card by having a card in his hands. There should be a facsimile of the card in the brochure so those at the dinner may follow the speaker's remarks. One important statement this speaker makes is to tell the number of pledges already received and their dollar amount.

The general hostess, assistant hostesses and table hostesses are responible for the attendance at the Loyalty Dinner. This group will contact every member-family and participating friends who are not yet members to invite them to attend the Loyalty Dinner.

There should be one hostess for every ten to fifteen member-families in the church. They will meet at least ten days before the Loyalty Dinner to receive instructions and choose the names of the families who will sit at their tables during the Loyalty Dinner. These names, as well as addresses and telephone numbers, will be on 3 × 5 cards.

Four or five days preceding the Loyalty Dinner the hostesses begin to telephone the families for whom they are responsible, to remind them of the dinner and get a confirmation of their plans to attend, even though they have already sent a reservation card. After a hostess has completed her calls she will report the results to the chairman of the hostess committee, stating how many will be attending.

The chairman of the committee will in turn give her report to the church office so all reservations may be completed before the deadline set by those serving the dinner.

At the Loyalty Dinner, the hostesses will be at the tables marked with their names. The families on her list will sit with her. She will make sure that everyone at her table has been introduced to each other, and will do all in her power to make the evening pleasant. At the close of the dinner, she will collect the prayer pledge cards and give them to the chairman of the hostesses.

This hostess committee is one of the most important in making the church feel as "one family." What they do will contribute greatly to the success of the canvass.

A SUGGESTED CALENDAR

At the same time selections are being made for the canvassing organization, a calendar should be prepared, giving in detail the schedule of the different activities. Dates should be chosen far enough in advance so there will be no conflict with other events. This will assure that the every-member canvass will be the major activity during that time. Following is the schedule for a six week canvass:

First Week:

Open canvass office
Mail pastor's letter
Leadership meeting
Publicity committee
Brochure to press
Selection of canvassers
Briefing of Sunday morning and church-school speakers
Pledge cards to press
Preparation of training materials

Second Week:

Meeting with hostess committee
Loyalty Dinner invitations mailed
Briefing of Loyalty Dinner speakers
First canvassers training session

Third Week:

Four canvassers training sessions
Brochure returned from press
Prepare pledge cards
Prepare and print Loyalty Dinner program and inserts

Fourth Week:

Loyalty Sunday
Two canvassers training sessions
Selection of pledge cards
Loyalty Dinner
Mailing to Loyalty Dinner absentees

Fifth Week:

Home visitations

Sixth Week:

Continuation of visitations
Pledge acknowledgments mailed
Post-canvass committee chosen and trained
Final-report meeting
Canvass analysis

This calendar will vary depending upon the size of the church, but in general this schedule may cover a membership of from 500 to 750 families.

SUGGESTIONS FOR CANVASSERS

Most canvassers approach visitations with some nervousness and hesitation, which is only natural, but let us see what a canvasser is asked to do.

First he is *not* asked to do something he cannot learn to do. He is *not* asking for money. He is not asked to change his personality nor to become a clever salesman. His work is neither a drudgery nor a burden. It is an important and enjoyable way of serving the Lord!

There are two essential things a canvasser needs in order to succeed at his task.

The first and greatest is *conviction*. He must believe that calling upon fellow church members is an important, almost a God-given task. This can not be done casually or impersonally. It must have meaning to be enjoyable and productive. The canvasser's conviction is expressed in his own act of sacrificial pledging.

The second thing the canvasser needs is *confidence and enthusiasm* that comes through adequate training. Enough training sessions are planned so every canvasser will be adequately oriented to the program. He is given sufficient information so he can adequately tell his story to the families he visits and answer questions intelligently. This training will give him confidence for his task. As the canvasser hears the program explained he will catch a vision of the proposed objective. Eventually he grasps its significance and develops an enthusiasm for it. Enthusiasm begets enthusiasm, thus it soon permeates the whole congregation.

Canvasser's should remember they are about the Lord's work. They are engaged in something about which they can and should pray. Pray for guidance, for wisdom, for God's blessing upon their efforts. Pray that through the canvass some fellow members in the church be brought closer to God.

To be of real help to others the canvasser should:

Know the story of his church and the canvass;
Know the needs which necessitate this canvass;
Know the plan to meet the needs;
Know the objective of the canvass, and
Know the methods of the canvass.

He will receive this knowledge through proper training by attendance at all training sessions.

CALLING IN THE HOME

The canvasser will make personal calls on prospective families. At the door he will announce his name *clearly*. When he states he is calling in the name of the church, he is heartily welcomed in almost every case. After getting into the home let him state his name again to other members of the family. This saves embarrassment to the one who met him at the door and cannot remember the visitor's name. When all amenities are over, the canvasser should get into the purpose of his call. He will discuss the full effect of the spiritual value of a sacrificial subscription. Always keep the conversation directed toward the giver. Once the canvasser takes a defensive position he is in a losing position.

Since these calls are made in the home, the entire family should participate in the decision on pledging. Make every effort to get the family together for the discussion. If there are external interruptions such as television, visitors, mealtime and such, do not give your presentation. Excuse yourself and make an appointment to return another time. The story you tell is much too important to share with any other activity. When the canvasser has the family together in the home, ask for a family prayer on the decision. It is an important decision for the family—more important to the family than to the church or to the canvass.

The canvasser must stress the need of the giver to make a sacrificial gift. Many a church member traces the beginnings of a real interest in his spiritual life to the time of decision when he first made an important, sacrificial gift to his church. More than money is being raised.

The canvasser may or may not telephone for an appointment. His time is valuable, and if phoning for an appointment will conserve it, do so unhesitatingly. However, it must be done tactfully and carefully, for a telephone conversation can easily move from an "appointment" discussion to a "solicitation" discussion and an easy opportunity for the prospective giver to say "no" or turn negative before the canvasser is able to talk to him personally. Be very careful in the use of the telephone.

The canvasser is seeking pledges only. Cash gifts frequently are cold-shoulders to the program. If a cash gift is offered, suggest that a weekly pledge be made instead. The difference between a cash gift and a subscription of sacrificial proportions will not only make a difference in the amount received by the church, but it will also make an even greater difference in the giver's spiritual interest in the coming years.

In case the family cannot come to a decision on the first visit, the canvasser keeps the pledge card in his pocket and arranges to return. The pledge card should never be left with the family. The family may hesitate to request the canvasser's second call, therefore, he should volunteer to make it. This is an important decision for the family and every encouragement should be given them.

Whether or not a pledge is received, always leave on a friendly note. The family visited is a part of the church and should never be made to feel that unless he pledges he is not wanted. A fitting closing note is, "I'll see you in church."

OUTCOME OF CANVASS

In addition to the various elements already discussed, such factors as size and age of the church and the type of canvass, whether for budget or expansion, will have a bearing on the final results. Despite these many factors it is, in most cases, possible to predict with some degree of accuracy what the final results will be. These predictions are based on the assumption that the canvass plan has been followed conscientiously and with enthusiasm.

In general, a building-fund canvass or a combined building-Fund and Current-Expense canvass will result in increases of 50 to 100 percent over previous total giving. A canvass for debt reduction or increased current expense budget have less emotional appeal and will result in increases of 30 to 70 percent over previous levels of giving.

Despite the sense of well being and, in some cases, complacency that follows a successful canvass, keep in mind that each new level of giving must be considered only a plateau from which to launch a new intensive stewardship effort in the future.

It is possible for a church to raise money for a new building or for debt reduction without professional help, or even without a canvass of any kind. However, a church should know its destination and should have a well-developed plan to reach its destination.

TWO BASIC FUNCTIONS

The church has two basic functions: (1) bringing Christ to its members and (2) bringing its members to Christ.

The latter requires action on the part of the members and certainly the signing of a generous or increased subscription is an indication that progress has been made in bringing that family closer to Christ. In other words, a canvass should be considered like a student's examination for each church family, with the generosity of their subscription representing the degree to which they have increased their spiritual interests.

The canvass is also a time for all of the church families to recognize the constant nearness of Christ—His proximity to them and every action in their lives—even to the point that He is looking over their shoulder while they are signing their cards, as He was watching the widow when she put in her mite.

As a final observation, we believe that if we were making ten rules for our children to follow, we would probably put the most important ones first. This must be equally true of the Ten Commandments, and yet as children we gloss over the first three, and concern ourselves with those about coveting and stealing.

Most of the troubles in the world today can be attributed to the flagrant breaking of the first three Commandments. Most people worship the dollar more than they do the Lord; most of us are idolizing it to the detriment of our physical, mental and spiritual lives.

Since we all recognize that interests follow dollars, and that all of us should try to live better balanced lives (physical, mental and spiritual), we need to compare how much we spend each year:

1. Feeding the physical $_____
2. Entertaining the mental $_____
3. Developing the spiritual $_____

The ultimate purpose of a fund-raising canvass is to strengthen the spiritual lives of the members of the church by bringing each family to a decision for sacrificial giving.

Chapter 8

MAKING A LOAN

INSTALLMENTS are the lifeblood of our national economy. Mortgaging the future has become a way of life. In fact, it has become so much a part of the way of life that insurance companies have found it profitable to insure purchasers on installments for a small premium to guarantee payment of the installments.

Installment buying and mortgaging future income makes it possible for many to have material things they would never have otherwise. It is most unusual for a young couple to start married life in their own home, completely furnished and debt free.

As this condition prevails for individuals and families, the same is true for universities, colleges, hospitals; for industries, governments and commerce; for scientific expansion, medical research and space probes. Everyone borrows from everyone else. This being true, it is impossible for the church to escape the need for special financing at some time or another.

CHURCHES NEED TO BORROW

There are few churches in the United States that have not borrowed money at some time. The ideal, of course, is for a church to pay as it goes. But there are few congregations able

to accumulate enough money to pay cash for a new building
or to remodel an old building.

The point of this chapter is that churches make loans, they
go into debt, and the loans must be repaid.

CHURCHES—POOR RISKS?

In some sections of our nation, lending institutions are reluctant to make loans to churches. For many years the church
was considered a poor risk.

Even as late as 1955 there was an aversion to church loans
by lending institutions. A church in which I was interested
wanted to borrow $100,000 for a building program. The offi-
cials of the church approached banks and savings and loan
associations but few of them showed any interest. Two lending institutions went so far as to ask for the plans and specifications to make a study of the building before giving any
answer to the request. Eventually one of them did make a
commitment. At that time, however, churches had not yet
proved they were worthy investments.

There are several reasons why this attitude prevails. First,
the paying record of some churches is not good. I was in a
church office one day when a florist came in on business.
During the course of his conversation I overheard him say
to the secretary, "We like to do business with this church
because we know our bills will be paid on time." This infers
there are some churches which do not pay their bills on time.
On another occasion I was with a pastor during a conversation with the wife of an electrical contractor. She told the
pastor her husband was pleased and surprised to receive a
check from the church so quickly. She explained further that
her husband was accustomed to sending bills for work done
for churches, then receiving a telephone call telling him the
bill was too much, or could he not give a discount, or would
he give part of the amount as a donation to the church. In
fact, it had become so embarrassing to him that he did not

care to do business with any of the churches in his community.

Further, an architect in southern Virginia has drawn the plans for many churches. He states that in seven of these instances the congregations occupy the buildings but still owe him money for his services. A church furniture company in Tennessee has had sad experiences in dealing with churches. They have had to wait months and at times years to be paid for furniture installed in church edifices. Another point of dissatisfaction is that many of the churches waited until the furniture was almost ready to be delivered, then changed their minds. The company could not collect for damages because the churches had nothing they could collect. These instances do not help the credit of churches.

Second, church buildings are one-use buildings. For the most part church edifices are of little use other than the purpose for which they are built. I recall a church building in California which was being sold because the congregation relocated. This was an imposing building, located on a valuable downtown corner in a city. Real estate agents had many prospects look at the building, but all refused to buy because it was too expensive to remodel the building into anything practical. The church building was eventually sold, torn down, and the corner used for other purposes.

I saw the same thing happen to a small church in a town in North Dakota. This congregation relocated, also. The old building was put on the market and sold. Years later the building stood abandoned, depreciating in value, deteriorating in appearance. The owner could find no use for the building.

Third, one-use buildings are poor security. If a congregation defaults, and the lending institution is forced to foreclose, it may be left with a white elephant. To take the building over with the expectation of disposing of it for some other purpose may terminate in a loss for the lender.

Fourth, when a church defaults, lenders are slow to bring legal action because of possible adverse public relations. I have heard officials of lending institutions say that foreclosure on a church could jeopardize the success of the institution because so many people are involved.

There is a small congregation in Virginia that had overreached itself. Leadership had not been good. The members were divided into several camps. Consequently, the loan payments were six months in arrears. The lending association had been very patient but finally threatened to foreclose. Only because of the intercession of denominational officials was the church saved from foreclosure and the lending association saved from embarrassment and ridicule.

Fifth, in Protestant churches the leadership is almost as changeable as the seasons of the year, and sometimes more frequent. Because this unstable condition exists in top leadership, lending institutions are reluctant to make loans. If this fluidity in leadership could be crystalized, this objection may be overcome. It seems to me there should be a rethinking of this problem among denominational leaders. Instead of fluctuating leadership in a local church, there could be a continuity of authority in the form of a denominational board endorsing the loan. This would alleviate the fear of men of integrity being replaced by men of irresponsibility.

For instance, a small church in southern Virginia wanted to borrow $60,000 for a new building. Several of the reliable members of the church approached a bank for the loan. These men had been in the community and in the church for some years. They were known for their integrity. The bank officials refused the money. Some time later other men of the church went to see the bankers. These men were prominent officials of the firms by whom they were employed. After a visit by these men the loan was granted. Such embarrassment could be avoided if authority were granted to some denominational official representing a denominational board, so he could go to a lending institution and make it known that the denomination as a whole is behind the men who make loans. The local church officials would do the borrowing, they would sign the notes, the congregation would be responsible for repayment, but the lending institutions would know that a denomination with all of its holdings would guarantee the payment.

This does not relieve the local church from its responsibilities. If there is a default the denomination can take some action to assure the lending institution that it will be paid. The local congregation then must repay the board for whatever expenditure it made. I believe whatever steps are taken in this direction will make the church a better credit risk than it is at present.

Sixth, it is a well-known fact that most churches have poor business practices. In many churches, there is careless bookkeeping and lack of responsibility both in incurring and paying bills. A joke with overtones of tragedy in it is that in some churches the bills are put in a hat and the first ones drawn out are paid. When no money remains the other bills are put back in the hat until the next month, when the procedure is repeated. It is hoped that in this way creditors will eventually be paid and, in the meantime, the church can continue its unbusinesslike conduct. One minister told me that after he had been in a new parish more than eight months, he found a $1,600-debt which had been due an architect more than two years. No one knew the debt existed.

There is a small church in a mining town in Pennsylvania where, after a worship service, the treasurer would put the offering in his pocket, take it home and put it in a box. When the monthly meeting of the official board was held he brought the box to the meeting. The money was poured out on a table and all the officials helped to count what had come in for the month. After the money was counted the bills were brought out. The money was divided as far as it would go.

After all the bills were paid and if some change was still left, the treasurer would say to the pastor, "Here, sir, is your salary for the month. I regret we cannot pay you the full amount, but we have to pay our other bills first."

Another church in Pennsylvania had a similar business plan. The treasurer collected whatever had been received in the offering during the worship service and took it home with him. No one ever knew how much was received. He paid the bills and he paid the pastor. It was not unusual for the pastor to go home with his pockets full of quarters and half-dollars on the day he was paid. There was never a deficit in this church because the treasurer made up any difference from his own income. There were no records and no one ever asked for an accounting. Such business practices do not make good credit risks.

CHURCHES—BIG BUSINESS

In spite of these credit risks, loans are made to churches. Churches are big business and many are good risks. The paying record of churches is improving, businesslike practices are being introduced, leadership is becoming more stable and millions of dollars are raised by churches every year. Churches are big business and lenders will listen if and when they are approached in the right manner and with the proper information.

Before church officials approach a lending institution they should prepare to vindicate their request. Be assured the lenders will ask many questions. They want assurances that the congregation is in a position to repay what they borrow. They will ascertain whether or not the congregation is borrowing too much. They will study the plans and specifications to make sure their money is going into a good structure. They are responsible for other people's money that has been entrusted to them, and they want to justify the trust that has been placed in them. Therefore, before approaching a lender, a financial data sheet should be prepared which can be left with every lending institution approached.

FINANCIAL DATA SHEET

In making up a Financial Data Sheet for the lending institution there are specific items of information which should be stated. These items may vary. I suggest these facts and figures:

First—the assets of the church, which include cash on hand, cash gifts or grants from denominational boards or other sources, value of land either appraised or actual and any other holdings which may be shown as assets.

Second—the amount needed; this includes the estimated cost of the building or remodeling substantiated by an architect or trustworthy contractor, the amount of the requested loan and, if there is a difference in these amounts, the source of the balance.

Third—membership growth, past, present and anticipated; such figures should cover five to eight years.

Fourth—history of contributions; this, also, should cover five to eight years, projected income one to three years, number of family units, number of units contributing, number of units not contributing and the average per unit.

Fifth—population trend in area of responsibility (This is particularly important if church is new; in older churches there should be knowledge of population trends for if there is no population growth a church should look closely at its building program.); this should show results of recent surveys, whether conducted on door to door basis by the church or as a result of consultation with utility companies, developers, contractors, etc., and should give geographical area of responsibility of church.

Sixth—project plans for future growth; include financial, membership, building, anticipated fund-raising efforts and any other information which will make a favorable impression on the lending institution.

Seventh—list responsible officers, names, addresses and their employment.

The following is a financial data sheet of a new congregation:

(Page One)
Springfield Methodist Church
Springfield, Virginia

I. *ASSETS:*
    A. Cash on hand $12,500.00
    B. Cash grant from denomination
        Church Extension Committee $20,000.00
            Total cash $32,500.00
    C. Appraised value of lot, owned
        free and clear by Springfield
        Methodist, Keene Mill Road &
        Spring Drive, Springfield, Va. $16,000.00
            Total cash and tangible assets $48,500.00

II. *PROPOSED CHURCH LOAN:*
    A. Architect's estimate of cost of
        unit $97,000.00
    B. Proposed loan $70,000.00
        Balance to be covered by Cash $27,000.00

    (Please refer to assets above)

(Page Two)

III. *MEMBERSHIP:*
    A. On Charter Sunday, March 14, 1954   137
    B. On March 6, 1955   335
    C. Estimated, January 1, 1956   600
    D. Estimated, January 1, 1957   850
    E. Estimated, January 1, 1958   1,000

IV. *HISTORY OF CONTRIBUTIONS:*

    A. For first year of church's
history, March 15, 1954
—March 6, 1955

       1. Estimated income $11,000.00

       2. Actual income $15,850.00

         (*Note:* This $15,850.00 contributed during first year was on regularly weekly pledges toward the budget. No building-fund canvass was necessary.)

    B. Estimated income for year
June 1, 1955—May 31, 1956 $35,360.00

    C. Number of family units
in church   155

    D. Number of family units contributing through pledges   124
(These family units consist of 275 adults and 18 youths, or a total of 293 of 335 members. Other members give but have not pledged.)

    E. Total value of pledges on hand
(52 weeks) $16,343.03

    F. Average per pledge $ 2.69

(Page Three)

V. *POPULATION TRENDS IN AREA:*

    A. Characterized by rapid growth of individually owned dwellings; developments include Crestwood, Yates Village, Lynnbrook, Beverly Forest, Springvale, Fairfax Park, Homewood, Bren Mar Park, Monticello Forest, Springfield Forest and others that are contemplated. Approximately 1,400 homes occupied at present.

    B. Recent surveys made by several church groups indicate about 25 percent of population are of Methodist preference.

    C. Area of church responsibility is bordered by Annandale Methodist Church and Franconia Methodist Church, both of which are more than three miles distant.

D. Estimated Population growth:

January 1, 1954	2,000
January 1, 1955	4,500
January 1, 1956	7,500
January 1, 1960	15,000

(Population estimate based on information furnished by construction companies and public utilities companies)

(Page Four)

VI. *PLANS FOR CHURCH GROWTH:*

A. The 137 members on Charter Sunday, underwrote, by pledges, $11,000 of a proposed annual budget of $15,600. This budget included $12,900 for the start of the first unit of our building.

B. The additional members received during the past ten months have contributed more than enough to cover the balance of the budget. (See Section IV, Page Two)

C. It is contemplated that regular annual budgets during the next two years will be underwritten so that in addition to covering operating expense there will be made possible substantial payments on the building loan and the purchase of required equipment for the new building. It is not anticipated that a special building-fund canvass will be necessary during this period.

D. It is thought that a special building-fund canvass may be undertaken during the year 1958 so that funds may be raised to construct the second unit of our building, the nave, in order to meet the needs of a much larger membership.

VII. *CHURCH BOARD OF TRUSTEES:*

The names of the trustees and their employment are included.

This information may be made as extensive as the church desires and presented in as impressive a manner as possible. Anything that will put the church in a good light should be done. A word of caution: Any information submitted should be such that it may be substantiated if necessary. False information would militate against the church and rightly so. Also, do not inflate figures on estimated progress. It is better to underestimate and be pleasantly embarrassed by success than to overestimate and be chagrined by failure.

WHY THE LOAN?

There are two principal reasons why a church makes a loan.

One, to pay current expenses and fulfill benevolence obligations: A congregation may come to the end of its fiscal year with obligations both to local creditors and to its connectional body. In order to enter the new year with all obligations met a short-term loan will be negotiated. Loans for current expenses and benevolences are discouraged. They do not relieve the church of any responsibility nor do they ease the financial burden. It is better to cut back on the church program, that would include benevolences, until the congregation is in a financial position to carry its share again.

Two, for capital improvements or building expansion: Most loans are in this category. Because the amount of money needed is greater than most congregations have in cash, it is necessary to borrow. To avoid too great an indebtedness at the time of building it is suggested that a congregation build its edifice in units rather than build all at one time. In building in units as the need arises, the congregation will be in debt for only the amount it is able to carry at the time. As membership grows, further units may be added. The debt will be spread over a larger number of member-families, thus avoiding a large loan by a few families. If this suggestion is followed, the architect should be asked to submit an overall plan. This will aid future building committees in developing a coordinated whole rather than a chaotic conglomeration.

HOW BIG THE LOAN?

How does a church determine what debt to incur? No debt should be so large as to interfere with the rest of the church program. It is easy for a church to refuse to contribute to benevolences because their own needs come first. The attitude is "once we have reduced our indebtedness we will give to missions." This is like cutting off the gas while expecting the engine to keep running. Sometimes the educational program is smothered, or salaries are kept too low for good leadership, or community service is nil, because a heavy debt must be paid first.

The members of a church in Pennsylvania had this very crippling experience some years ago. They built a large, modern edifice, including both worship and educational space. It was much more than the small congregation needed. They went into debt for thousands of dollars at a local banking institution.

For a time the congregation made its mortgage payments but had no money for any other program. Because of the heavy debt, prospective members went elsewhere. Some members were living on limited income and unable to contribute. Fewer and fewer members were bearing the financial burden. Eventually the congregation was able to pay only the interest on the loan and frequently this was not paid. The denominational leaders sent young ministers to the church to revitalize it. These young men remained two years, no more than three, then moved out. The church suffered; the program was stifled, and the Kingdom of God had an unproductive vineyard. This church has always stood out in my mind as an agonizing example of what may happen when there is too much debt.

Several formulas have been proposed by authorities in this field to help guide churches in determining what is a safe debt. Some church-extension leaders have given a threefold formula:

First—take an amount equal to $200 per church family (It is important to note this figure is based on *family* not member.);

Second—take an amount equal to 40 percent of the cost of
   construction;

Third—take an amount equal to three and one-half times the
   annual budget;

Add these three items together and divide by three. This will
   give an average amount which may be safely carried.

Others state that a church should not borrow more than 50
percent of the total cost of construction. In fact, many institutions will not loan much more than this amount. Some
insurance companies may go as high as 70 or 80 percent.
Such a large loan is discouraged, however, because of the
heavy burden it puts on the church in repayment.

Still others suggest it is better if the church waits until it
has at least 50 percent of the needed money on hand before
applying for a loan. Then before the total amount is needed,
make an effort to add another 25 percent to what is already
on hand. It is obvious that with 75 percent of the needed
money in cash, the remaining debt would not militate against
the program of the church and would certainly stimulate the
membership to greater stewardship.

There is one caution sign on the road to borrowing and it
states: Do not overburden the congregation!

SOURCES FOR BORROWING

Where do we go to borrow money? Most churches do not
have rich uncles or angels. On rare occasions one finds a
wealthy member, or family, willing to make a loan for an
expansion program. Unless the member or family is devoutly
Christian and humble with their wealth, such loans should
be discouraged. In most instances when these members make
such a large loan to a church they exert too much pressure
in determining policies. Frequently they tell what to do for
benevolences, education, and go so far as to tell the minister
what to preach. Such loans will help bring ruin to a church

—fast! If such an offer is made, make certain all terms are spelled out explicitly and plainly, otherwise let the church officials say, "Get thee behind me, Satan."

There is another side to this. Some families willingly and with good intent make a loan to the church. They do not want their names mentioned. The news will out, however, which brings embarrassment to the family. For instance, one family that benefited a church in this way told me they had to withdraw from any official position, because whenever they expressed an opinion, others in the church would remain silent fearing if they opposed what was said they would offend the wealthy family. This family was too humble and too gracious to want such catering, and so withdrew.

If we do not borrow from wealthy members, then we turn to various commercial lending institutions. We think first of banks. For years banks were the main source for lending money. However, because bankers are usually conservative, and because they are limited by law in the amount to be loaned to churches, some church officials are reluctant to approach banks. I have always found bankers quite understanding and very willing to discuss loans to churches. They should be contacted.

In more recent years savings-and-loan or building-and-loan associations have become recognized as lenders to churches. Comparatively speaking, these institutions are newcomers to the money market. However, the success they have had and the millions of dollars that have been invested with them have put them in a position where they are willing to make loans to churches for building purposes. Many of these associations will loan as much as two-thirds of the estimated cost of construction. The officers of these institutions, just as officers of banks, are men interested in their communities. Give serious consideration to discussing your need with them.

Insurance companies are custodians of much wealth in this country. Many of these companies make loans to churches. Some of these companies make a higher percentage loan than either of the other sources. In most cities and towns large insurance companies have representatives, who may be approached with inquiries.

We mention again the sale of church bonds as a source of borrowing money for church expansion. This is covered in detail in chapter 6.

A new source for loans has more recently developed in the larger denominations. The Methodist Church, for instance, a few years ago instituted a new church extension loan fund. This fund began with several hundred thousand dollars. The news spread rapidly and churches of all sizes made applications for loans. In one action, the directors of the fund authorized loans totaling $466,500 to churches in New Jersey, New York, Indiana, Illinois, Louisiana, Texas, Utah, Washington and California. In one 12-month period the amount of loans increased from $1,479,079 to $3,959,000.

The fund has become a multimillion-dollar business. It is supported by investments from local churches, hospitals, annual conference agencies, general boards, homes for children, and individuals.

Make inquiry into what your denomination is doing about this.

There is one other source for money which should be investigated by churches. There are individual firms (many of them in the southwestern part of our country), which have money to loan specifically to churches. These companies, serving religious congregations only, have been the means of providing millions of dollars to churches for capital improvement all over the United States.

The officers of a congregation needing to borrow money will have little or no trouble finding sources for funds so long as they can prove they are worthy of the investment.

TYPE OF LOANS

What kind of loans are made? Basically there are only two categories: long-term and short-term. However, in each of these categories there are both secured and unsecured loans.

For a capital-improvement loan, the most likely type would be the secured long-term loan. The long-term loan runs five years or longer. Since this usually involves a large investment, the lending institution would assign the church property as collateral.

The second type is the unsecured long-term loan. It would be most unusual for a lending institution to make such a loan. The risk is too great and could mean disaster to the institution making the loan.

A third type is the secured short-term loan. This loan is one which would be repaid in three to five years. Here again, the collateral is usually the church property.

The fourth type of loan is the unsecured short-term loan. There are times when these loans are justified. For instance, if a church is in an area where seasonal employment determines the income of the church, short-term loans may be necessary. In rural areas the Fall is obviously the season of the year when the church thrives financially. In summer resort areas, the church may find itself in a slump during the cold weather but flourishing during the summer. However, expenditures take place all year round. Thus, in order to meet some of its obligations, unsecured short-term loans are made. They should be for not more than one year. However, they may run as long as five years.

If the loan is a real short-term loan, such as thirty or sixty days, then a promissory note may be sufficient and may be renewable by mutual agreement.

LET'S PAY IT ALL BACK!

In considering the repayment of a loan, several things should be considered.

First, do not make the loan for too many years. Long-term loans for churches should be discouraged. Over a period of 25 or 30 years, the interest is staggering. This vindicates the saying, "We used to do things for posterity, but now we do things for ourselves and leave the bill to posterity." Churches should keep their loans to 10 years, no longer than 15. The payments are higher but there is great savings on interest. Furthermore, in shorter time the church will be in a position to give more support to other areas of the church program.

Second, in borrowing, the church should incorporate in all legal documents the privilege of prepayment without penalty. This gives the church the right to pay as much more as possible above the regular payments, or even to pay the debt in full, any time before the expiration date. There is always the possibility that a congregation may receive a bequest, or the income of the church may increase, making possible early payment.

Also, because of a changing economy and the fluidity of the money market, it is possible that a church may find itself in a position to borrow the money from another source at lower interest. Thus, it is able to pay off the earlier loan. Get the prepayment clause in your loan!

HOW MUCH FOR DEBT REDUCTION?

What percentage of the total church financial program should be set aside for debt reduction? Once more several factors must be considered: the size of the budget, the size of the debt and the amount of other obligations. It is quite obvious that if a church has an annual budget of $70,000 and the mortgage payment takes $40,000 of this amount, the church is in difficulty both in financial and spiritual matters. If this amount must be raised for debt reduction, the congregation should consider refinancing to ease the burden.

It has been suggested that no more than 35 percent of the

total budget should be used for debt retirement. Sharpen your pencil and figure carefully!

WAS SHAKESPEARE RIGHT?

Shakespeare wrote, "Neither a borrower, nor a lender be; for a loan oft loses both itself and friend; and borrowing dulls the edge of husbandry. He apparently had had a sad experience. Perhaps he had made a loan and was not paid back, or he tried to collect and lost both his money and his friend.

When a church borrows money, it should be with every intention of repaying, and let us be grateful that few churches go into bankruptcy. Churches need not be ashamed to be borrowers—in fact, unless they are, they may find themselves cutting programs short; silencing their witnessing, and stifling their progress. Borrowing need not dull the edge of husbandry. On the contrary, it has made many congregations better stewards for God.

Chapter 9

CHURCH FINANCES— WHOSE RESPONSIBILITY?

I APPROACH this question with mixed emotions. Before I became a pastor I was a layman—just as all pastors were. The story is told of three young priests who were at a football game between Notre Dame and Southern Methodist. Each time Southern Methodist made a good play the priests stood and cheered. A curious spectator approached the young men and asked why it was they were cheering for a Methodist school against Notre Dame. One of the priests replied, "Before we were priests we were Texans." So, every pastor was a layman.

I can remember that as a layman I took the attitude that the pastor should raise the money for the church. Let him devise plans and schemes to get money from people. After all, it is his church. Now looking at it from the point of view of the pastor, I wonder how I could have entertained such thoughts.

The quickest answer as to who is responsible for fund raising is that both pastor and laymen have their places in this important phase of the work of the church. They do not eliminate one another. They supplement each other. They pool their energies and work as a team.

150

THE PASTOR'S THORN IN THE FLESH

Many pastors avoid this part of church administration. They have an aversion to the materialistic aspect of church finances. Their attitude is that money is "filthy lucre"; it is the "root of all evil." Others are not quite so brash in their statements. Nevertheless, they feel that raising money interferes with their "spiritual" work.

I have had pastors tell me they never look at the financial records of their church. They do not want to know what their people pledge nor what they give. These pastors state they are the servants of all the people—poor or wealthy. Sometimes those who need him most are those who cannot afford to give to the church. If he has knowledge of what people are giving, he may be biased in his ministry and cater only to those who are financially supporting the program.

These pastors state that the financing of the church is the responsibility of the layman. These men are more accustomed to dealing with the mundane things of life. They know how to talk to businessmen; they know where to get the best bargains; they know how to raise funds. There is an interrelationship between the pastor and the layman, to be sure, but the division of labor between the spiritual and the material is important. Let the layman take care of the material and the pastor is free to care for the spiritual. This is the expression of many pastors.

I cannot accept this idea, completely. A pastor ought to know whether his people are financially supporting the program of the church just as he knows whether or not they are attending the worship services or prayer meetings. To be lax in stewardship of money is as spiritually dangerous for a Christian as it is to be careless in his prayer life. A person who does not financially support the church may be put in an official position where he may interfere with the whole program of the church. A pastor ought to be aware of this.

Furthermore, if a pastor allows his knowledge of giving by his members to interfere with his ministry to them, then I maintain there is immaturity in his spiritual and mental growth. Taking offense at the lack of financial support by a member indicates the pastor is wearing his feelings too close to the surface. He unites himself to the church to the degree that any action for or against the church is an action for or against himself. He must be bigger than this!

Church fund raising is a thorn in the flesh to many pastors. In spite of what is written above, I sympathize with them.

THE IDEAL PASTORATE

Many pastors would consider the ideal parish one in which they did not have to be concerned about the finances of the church. If they could go about the tasks for which they are specifically prepared, making visitations, counseling, conducting worship or teaching, or if they could devote time to studying and meditating, this would make the perfect situation. However, church finances are closely related to all other functions of the church. Stewardship is a vital part of Christian growth. Fund raising cannot be ignored by the pastor.

I do not advocate making the pastor a professional fund raiser. There are so many areas of responsibility for which he should be prepared in our day but seminaries do not have the time to train him. To make him a fund raiser would add to an already burdensome load. I do believe, however, that he should be acquainted with many of the practices and procedures of church fund raising so that he in turn may train his laymen if necessary. Fund raising is time-consuming. It requires the cooperation of many people. Therefore, I believe the pastor has a definite place in fund raising and cannot stand by while others assume the task. There is no ideal pastorate.

WHAT DOES THE PASTOR DO?

The pastor's most important role in fund raising is that of being spiritual leader. Laymen appreciate having their pastor at hand when they are involved in an every-member visitation or when they are discussing church finances. Whether the idea is good or not, laymen think of their pastor as having a special relationship to God. They believe the pastor should be able to give a word of encouragement under all circumstances and be able to offer an appropriate prayer when asked to do so.

To my mind this is one area where the pastor may show his faith in God. If the church is facing a financial squeeze the pastor should be the leader to reveal that he believes God will help in all circumstances. The pastor may be concerned, he may be as anxious as any of his leaders; however, if his laymen are to have courage and hope in such circumstances it will come as they see it revealed in their pastor, their spiritual leader. This could be the greatest contribution the pastor may make.

As spiritual leader, the pastor will sometimes lead in spirit only. If he has knowledge of the technique of fund raising, let him share it but remain inconspicuous. He will give the benefit of his experience, he will be free with his know-how, he will be available for counsel, but he will remain in the background. The laymen will feel the pastor's interest even when he is not present. They will be aware of his understanding and devotion at all times.

The pastor will know the goals of the church better than anyone else. In all probability the desired goals are a result of his vision and of the inspiration he has given others to see them. He knows the heights he wants the church to reach. He has seen them many times in his own mind. Now he must keep these goals before the laymen, arouse their enthusiasm to make them as enthusiastic as he is, and urge them to victory.

A church in one community had been struggling for years with an inadequate building, insufficient funds and a lackadaisical attitude. Everyone knew something should be done but no one set about to do it. A new pastor was assigned. He had been on the field only a short time when he began to discuss the needs with people in the congregation. Within a matter of months the wheels were in motion to take care of the building needs. The members of the church began to show a new spirit about things. Attendance at the worship services increased and the whole program of the church had a rebirth. The whole difference was in the enthusiasm, the vision and optimism of the pastor.

The pastor will help discover and develop lay leadership. In my own experience I have seen churches revitalized during an every-member visitation. It is truly a spiritual revival. In some churches men with outstanding ability have often been allowed to sit on the side lines. Their talents have been wasted in idleness. Since the pastor is usually the best acquainted with the congregation he can suggest such men for places of leadership in the visitation organization. After they have been enlisted, the pastor can help develop them by welcoming them, encouraging them, instructing them and giving them companionship.

The president of a large organization was a member of a community church. The pastor noticed that this man seldom attended worship services or took any part in the church program. The pastor began to make inquiry about it and learned that an injustice had really been done the man. He had been a member of the property committee and had been assigned such duties as cleaning windows, replacing broken glass, changing burned-out light bulbs and, occasionally, sweeping the floor. This man was not conceited nor did he feel these jobs were too menial. However, he was not going to do these jobs around the church when he had men in his employ whom he pàid to do these tasks. Here was outstanding leadership ability that was being wasted. Unless the pastor had made inquiry this man might have sat on the side lines doing nothing. When challenged with a major task he rose to the occasion.

The pastor alone is responsible for stewardship sermons which will point out the Christian use of money. This is difficult for many pastors. They have an inner repulsion on this subject. They do not want to be known as "money grubbers." They refrain from making the pulpit an auction block. They want to avoid hounding members with sermons on money. Nevertheless, there is a need to develop a Christian attitude to the use of money by church members. Sermons on the proper use of money cannot be ignored by pastors.

Church fund raising should be interpreted in its relation to God through the Christ. The pastor should be able to do this better than anyone else, if he himself has the right attitude toward money and its use for good. Although this was discussed more fully in chapter 1, let it be repeated here: When money is raised for the church, the giver is asked to give more than dollars and cents, he is asked to give himself to God through the church. The giver's money represents the giver. Let the pastor keep this interpretation before his congregation and in time they know they are involved in something greater than supporting a church budget.

A young pastor had been appointed to a church in a suburb of Philadelphia. He had an attractive nave, fine educational facilities and a small staff. His congregation was made up of people in the middle- and upper-middle-class group. It did not take him long to discover that the church was not living up to its financial potential either for local needs or for the benevolence program. He began to preach stewardship sermons. At least once a quarter he would lift up the stewardship of possessions. At first there was some resistance but eventually the members realized they were holding out on God. They began to give, the church grew in membership and financial support. Year after year they invited the pastor back and, in order to show their devotion to him, the congregation sent him and his wife to the Holy Land, all expenses paid—round trip, of course. Stewardship sermons are the prerogative of the pastor; no one can take his place here.

All of these suggestions are important in a fund-raising program. They help make spiritual what could be a very materialistic thing. These are the tasks the pastor is best trained to do in church fund raising.

It seems to me a pastor would want to have a part in fund raising for his church, to share in the feeling of accomplishment after the goal has been reached, to rejoice with his laymen after successfully completing the project.

One evening I sat in the closing meeting of a successful every-member visitation. Rejoicing filled the air; the atmosphere was full of victory. One layman after the other rose to tell what the canvass had meant to him. The canvass leaders who had given so much of their time were so jubilant they could hardly contain themselves. During all this time the pastor of the church sat to one side enjoying the evening as much as anyone. The success of the canvass had meant so much to him and the program he was stressing. After the laymen had had their say they turned to their pastor and with great pride asked him to share with them his feelings. These laymen did not want their pastor left out. They had appreciated his help and encouragement. Although the hour seemed to be theirs, they wanted to share it with him. They rejoiced because he was with them in this glorious hour.

It seems to me that any pastor who closes the door on such an exhilarating experience because he is more concerned about spiritual things is depriving himself of a rebirth in his ministry.

WHAT DOES THE LAYMAN DO?

In answering this question, what does the layman do in church fund raising, I want to pay tribute to the laymen who have been my co-laborers during the years of my ministry. All during the years there have been laymen who have assumed the major role in church fund raising. They have supported the church liberally and faithfully. However, there is a group of laymen to whom I pay a special tribute. These are the men who have labored with me and encouraged me in my present pastorate. Together we started a church from nothing but a vacant field and no members to the place where there is now a building worth almost $700,000 and a membership of 2,300. Through their cooperation we have watched the budget grow from $0 to $140,000 per year. This has taken place in less than ten years.

Many of these men assumed responsibilities about which they knew little or nothing as far as fund raising was concerned. Year after year, financial programs, and, several times, building programs were suggested which would have been staggering to some. But these men always took the attitude "under God we can do it." They were not rich in money but they were rich in faith. Once these men have seen a need, they have moved ahead unselfishly to meet the challenge. My wish is that all pastors were surrounded with such devoted laymen.

The laymen should plan the financial program of the church. Budget hearings are scheduled to which committee chairmen are invited to present the financial needs for their part of the church program. Each dollar requested should be vindicated, not because there is a desire to be mercenary, but because the money belongs to God and diligent stewardship is essential. After the hearings, the requests are compiled and prepared for presentation to the proper official body and eventually to the congregation for its support. Laymen work with laymen in planning.

After the congregation has underwritten the budget, the laymen manage the finances. A group of laymen are responsible for counting the weekly offerings either while the worship service is being held or immediately thereafter. If counted during the worship service, then the service should be "piped" into the office or room where the men are working so they may have the benefit of the service.

In some churches a staff member is responsible for counting the offering Monday morning. Unless there is a strong and secure place to keep the money overnight, this practice should be discouraged because of the danger of burglary. It may be possible to arrange to place the money in the night depository of a local bank and count the money at the bank next day. Whichever method is used, it is definitely the laymen's responsibility.

The laymen are responsible for distribution of funds. The treasurer should have the authority to pay all items as they become due, if they are budgeted items. Of course, because an item is in the budget, it does not follow that the money is there to be spent. It is good business procedure to appoint several laymen as a budget control committee to work with the treasurer in determining the distribution of funds on an equitable basis. Special expenditures or nonbudgeted items should be resubmitted to the official body for action.

Certainly no pastor should assume responsibility for expenditure of church funds. It lends itself to character defamation. It indicates, too, the pastor's inability, or lack of desire, to delegate responsibility. It may indicate that the pastor assumes too much responsibility.

The laymen should make certain the congregation, as a whole, is kept informed of the financial position of the church. An account should be made to the congregation of the amount of money which has been received and how much has been expended. If there is a surplus, it should be made known. If there is a need, this should be made known. This information may be made available through the church bulletin, newsletter or, occasionally, a congregational letter written specifically for this purpose. Individual statements should be sent to the members to keep them informed of their giving.

New members should be contacted by laymen as soon as possible to solicit their financial support of the church. As indicated earlier in this book, it is never too soon to talk to new members about the finances of the church. Properly trained laymen can do this job tactfully and successfully.

The every-member visitation, whether annual or biannual, is definitely the responsibility of laymen. As indicated above, the minister will be available for help, for inspiration and for guidance, but it is the laymen who spark the visitations and carry the work load. In fact, this is one of the finest opportunities for laymen of the church to become acquainted with other members of the congregation. Laymen working with laymen strengthen each other.

Altogether there are three areas of responsibility for the laymen in church fund raising: planning the budget, preparing the budget and underwriting the budget.

HELPFUL HINTS FOR BOTH PASTORS AND LAYMEN

When budgets are set, they should be large enough to challenge the congregation to do more than it has ever done before. To have a budget that is easily within reach of the membership does not call for spiritual growth nor sacrificial giving. The financial officer of one church told me they had met their budget every year for years. All obligations had been met and the church was in excellent financial position. At the same time he volunteered the information that they had not had an every-member visitation for at least five years.

The members gave the same year after year and everyone was happy. I do not believe there is much reason for rejoicing in this situation. Regardless of how well a church may be doing financially, there is much more it can do and there is a greater challenge it can make to its membership. A budget should challenge!

Budgets should be challenging so people will be motivated to change their habits of giving. Most families have developed the habit of giving the least they can. It is a habit they keep most of their life. However, a church budget should be such that it will call for sacrifice on the part of its members to change from giving the least they can to more than they are able. Once this habit has been changed it is the responsibility of pastor and laymen to continue to challenge so the new habit will be continued. To do otherwise is to fail.

The latter idea calls for further consideration. Our motive is not merely to get more money—the ultimate goal is to transfer this commitment to the giving of self. After all, this is the greater stewardship. In all appeals for money there is the overriding appeal for the giver himself.

ONENESS CREATED

Another benefit arising from a challenging budget is the sense of oneness created in a church. In raising the budget, laymen call in the homes of laymen, friendships are created, members are brought closer together, the purpose of the church is explained and, as people give, they feel more a part of that to which they have given. The church becomes a "family" indeed.

It is important that both laymen and pastor have a proper perspective of fund raising as it relates to stewardship. Unfortunately stewardship is frequently taught in a church as if it meant use of money only. Stewardship is the larger circle of which fund raising is a smaller circle. Stewardship is a way of life which encompasses all of life. It is unfortunate when stewardship is used in a narrower sense, when it is subverted to the ulterior use of raising money for a church.

For instance, a finance committee found itself facing a financial crisis. After some deliberation it was decided to have a month of stewardship emphasis. Letters, brochures and lay-talks were prepared. For four weeks the congregation was soundly oriented to stewardship. However, the whole effort was misdirected, for the only emphasis was on giving money to the church. At the end of the four weeks the finance committee had raised a few more dollars for the church, they had aroused the ire of some of the members, and no one had become a better steward of life.

Laymen and pastors should be aware of the great spiritual values that come from a challenging budget and well-directed every-member visitation. Many canvasses have had the same spiritual results as if a revival had been conducted in the church. In fact, a few of the same patterns may be evident: request for prayer time by the congregation, well-developed plans, good organization. However, a fund-raising canvass is not a revival, so there will be differences in approach. The end result may be a spiritual awakening for the church as a whole and for individuals in the church.

I remember a professor of a college in Canada who staunchly opposed an every-member canvass in his church. He spoke against it and voted against it. As the organization was being set up he was asked to take part. He came in reluctantly but with the promise that he would do his best. When the canvass was over this man was one of the first to state it was the best thing to happen to him in many years. His whole attitude toward the church had been changed. He was a better Christian.

THE GIVER'S NEED

If spiritual qualities are desired through a fund-raising canvass, then it is futile to direct attention to the church's needs only. Even in the post-budget canvass the needs of the church are of least importance. To be sure, a given number of dollars are needed but this is not the main emphasis. The most important element in fund raising is the need of the giver to give. Let the emphasis be put here and not only will the money be given, but the giver will be spiritually benefited.

I overheard two men discussing their philosophy on giving to the church. One man said he liked to give to the church until it hurt. The other man disagreed with this, he said he liked to give to the church until it felt good. The latter man went down to his house blest. He had learned the giver's need: the need to give himself.

THE CHURCH GIVES

The church which sets its goal to meet only its own needs, is beginning to vegetate. When a congregation becomes more concerned about paying its utility bills, keeping its property in good condition, providing comfort for itself, that church is the fig tree which puts out pretty blossoms but bears no fruit. The truly great church is one in which there is greater concern for others than for self. The money it raises is to be given away, not to be kept. And it raises as much to be given away as it does for its own purposes.

There is a downtown church in Alexandria, Virginia, that suffered all the problems a downtown church suffers. Its members were moving into the suburbs. Those who worshiped there traveled many miles and passed many churches each Sunday. Finances were short. In order to perform a downtown ministry, the church needed to enlarge its facilities. When the pastor mentioned the need, the officials immediately opposed him. They could not afford what he asked, they said. Seeing that he was being defeated in this project, the pastor then proposed that the congregation establish a new church south of the city and give both their moral and financial support to the project. The officials of the church adopted this idea. Money began to be raised for the project. The new congregation was established. Many of the members of the mother church united with the new one. Then a miracle began to happen. Instead of the downtown church suffering from the loss of members and undergoing greater financial strain, the membership increased, finances were better than they had ever been, and the building project the pastor had proposed earlier was acted on favorably. A church that gives . . . grows!

When a church raises money for others—or with the purpose of giving it away, then fund raising is taken out of the realm of begging. For a congregation to see its own needs, to emphasize only these needs in fund raising, is like a beggar standing along the road of life with a tin cup in his hands taking whatever people will give and being pleased with the results. A church that asks—then gives—is not a beggar.

IN SUMMARY

Church fund raising is more than the responsibility of the pastor, and it is more than the responsibility of the laymen; it is a combined and united effort of prayers, work and giving. After such a united effort, all can justly rejoice in the success of their accomplishment for the glory of God and the help of their fellowmen. For laymen to do it alone is to deprive themselves of the companionship of a strong spiritual resource person, their pastor. For the pastor to attempt to do it alone is to cheat the laymen of an opportunity to grow in Christian living and giving.

BIBLIOGRAPHY

Bramer, John C., *Efficient Church Business Management*. Philadelphia: The Westminster Press, 1950.

Briggs, Edwin A., *A Modern Point of View on Tithing*. 1200 Davis Street, Evanston, Illinois: 1963.

Crossland, Weldon, *A Planned Program for the Church Year*. Nashville: Abingdon Press, 1951.

———, *Church Building Finance*. National Council of the Churches of Christ in the U.S.A. 1951.

Dobbins, Gaines S., *Building Better Churches*. Nashville: Broadman Press, 1947.

———, *The Churchbook*. Nashville: Broadman Press, Nashville, 1951.

Gamble, Charles W. and Winona, *How to Raise Money*. New York: Association Press, 1942.

Hale, Ashley, *Creative Fund-Raising*. Chicago: Wells Organizations, 1952.

Harral, Stewart, *Public Relations for Churches*. Nashville: Abingdon Press, 1945.

———, *Successful Letters for Churches*. Nashville: Abingdon Press, 1946.

Holt, David R., III, *Handbook of Church Finance*. New York: The Macmillan Company, 1960.

Leach, William H., *Handbook of Church Management*. Englewood Cliffs, N.J.: Prentice-Hall, Inc., 1958.

Lumley, Arthur W., *Raising Money for Church Building Projects*. Nashville: Abingdon Press, 1954.

Pendleton, Othniel, Jr., *New Techniques for Church Fund Raising.* New York: McGraw-Hill Book Co., Inc., 1955.

Pleuthner, W. A., *More Power For Your Church.* New York: Farrar, Straus and Young, 1952.

Powell, Luther P., *Money and the Church.* New York: Association Press, 1962.

Thompson, T. K., *Stewardship in Contemporary Theology.* New York: Association Press, 1960.

Ward, Hiley H., *Creative Giving.* New York: The Macmillan Company, 1958.

Magazines and Pamphlets

Analysis of the Problem of Inadequate Church Income Based on Motivation Research. American Institute of Motivation Research, California, 1961.

Church Administration. Monthly. The Sunday School Board, Southern Baptist Convention, 127 Ninth Avenue, North, Nashville 3, Tennessee.

Church Management. Monthly. Church Management, Inc., 2491 Lee Boulevard, Cleveland Heights 18, Ohio.

Your Church. Quarterly. The Religious Publishing Company, 122 Old York Road, Jenkintown, Pennsylvania.

For further information or consultative assistance on wills, endowments, etc., the following organizations and persons are suggested and recommended:

Department of Stewardship and Benevolence,
National Council of Churches of Christ in the U.S.A.
T. K. Thompson, Executive Secretary
475 Riverside Drive, New York 27, New York

Committee on Gift Annuities
Charles W. Baas, Chairman
450 Park Avenue, New York 22, New York

Sydney Prerau, Attorney-at-Law and Philanthropic Counselor
155 East 44th Street, New York 17, New York

Institute for Philanthropic Planning, Inc.
Walter Mortensen, Executive Director
645 Madison Avenue, New York 21, New York

Family Films, Hollywood, California (producers of two motion
pictures on wills: *Treasures in Heaven and God's Will Through
Yours*).

INDEX